JUPITER MOSMAN

THE GOLD DISCOVERER AT CHARTERS TOWERS

AN ACCOMMODATION

MICHAEL BRUMBY

We acknowledge the Traditional Owners of the land on which we publish books, the Quandamooka people and pay our respects to Elders past, present and emerging.

Published by:
Boolarong Press
38/1631 Wynnum Road
Tingalpa Qld 4173
Australia.
www.boolarongpress.com.au

First published 2022

A catalogue record for this book is available from the National Library of Australia

ISBN: 9781922643216 (paperback)

Typeset by Boolarong Press in Amiri 12pt

Cover design by Boolarong Press
Front cover image: Jupiter Mosman, 1942, Ross Jamieson Collection
Back cover image: Blanket Day, Charters Towers Court House, 1889, Arthur Bailey photographer, Charters Towers Archives

Printed and bound by Watson Ferguson & Company, Tingalpa, Australia

for James

OTHER WRITINGS BY
MICHAEL BRUMBY

A Century of Playing the Game: The First Hundred Years of Schooling at Richmond Hill State School, Charters Towers, 1895–1995. (1995)

Muskets and Mantlets: A Brief history of the Life and Times of the Charters Towers Rifle Range 1885-1995. (1996)

Goldfield Ashes 50th Anniversary Souvenir Programme. (1997)

One Square Mile: Re-Discovering the Buildings and the Life of Mosman, Gill and Bow Streets Charters Towers, North Queensland. (1997)

Beyond the Bin. (1998)

Millchester State School: A Celebration of 125 Years Including the Closed Schools of Queenton, Mount Leyshon, The Broughton and King's Gully. (1999)

125 Years of Ravenswood State School. (1999)

A History of the Charters Towers Civic Club 1900–2000. (2000)

Charters Towers: New Century New Nation 1901. (2001)

Lager to Library: A History of the Excelsior Hotel 1887–2003. (2003)

Charters Towers 1887: Celebrating the Photographic Work of Carey Jamieson Allom and Arthur Rudolph Bailey. (2004)

A History of the Former Ambulance Building Charters Towers. (2005)

Charters Towers: A Street Walk. (2006)

Charters Towers: A History in Buildings. (2006)

The Natives and the Buffs: The Buffalo Hall at Charters Towers 1894–2008. (2008)

Charters Towers: People and Places. (2010)

Streets. (2011)

Charters Towers: World Connections. (2012)

Towers Players 1962–2012. (2012)

Black to Gold. (2014)

'The World' and the Great World War. (2017)

Towers Hill: Unearthed Secrets (2021)

CONTENTS

INTRODUCTION

Mrs Kenny from Kajabi and Mrs May Considine from Mount Isa were pictured in The Northern Miner following the opening of Jupiter Mosman Arcade in Charters Towers on 20th June 1980. This was the first shopping arcade erected in Gill Street Charters Towers which was named in honour of Jupiter whom locals claimed discovered the first gold at Charters Towers. The women were guests at the opening, saying their father was "Archie Mosman, the brother of Hugh who adopted young Jupiter. Archer [sic] was an early landowner in the north." (TNM: 07/06/1980; TDB: 06/06/1980) Until then, I had read and understood that Jupiter had no family and hence held no ties as he had never married.

Jupiter's western family re-emerged in 1997, when a giant boomerang was unveiled in Lissner Park on the 25th May 1997 to honour him as the discoverer of the gold at Charters Towers. The local Aboriginal community played an active part in recognizing Jupiter, along with members of the extended families of Mrs Kenny and May Considine whom I met. But this time their connection to Jupiter was clarified when they said, "We don't belong to Jupiter. We're Archie's family. He was Hugh Mosman's brother." (TB: 26/05/1997)

I was curious to know more, eventually establishing that Archibald Frederick Mosman lived and worked in the west of Queensland for most of his life. He had worked for Alexander Kennedy at Noranside near Boulia in 1879. Kennedy put Archie in charge of the 3,000 bullocks who got them to Victoria in good condition after four months droving. But in 1883 Archie Mosman joined the Native Police aged 37 when he commenced duties at Burke River (Boulia). He left the force in 1890 and took up White Hills Station to the north of Cloncurry: country described as "undoubtedly the roughest piece of country it has been my lot to inspect. It is practically all rough, rocky hills growing spinifex and very lightly timbered with mountain gum." (White Hills Part 1 - 14/01/1927) This was something I could vouch for after visiting the place in 2000, on a quest to know more about Archie and his family and their connection to Jupiter and of course to Charters Towers.

I learnt from the family that Archie Mosman formed a relationship with a young Indigenous girl from Lake Nash who was known as Kitty. In 1895, the first of their four daughters was born at White Hills. This was May Calton Mosman, who was followed by Aprilla 'Tilly,' Nora and Junella. Archie married Kitty in 1911. He signed the certificate while Kittie made her mark. Kitty declared her father was Barney but did not name her mother. Archibald Mosman was 65 and Kitty was 40. Seven years later Archie was dead. But not so his legacy.

Materially, Archibald Frederick Mosman was one six for-life beneficiaries of brother Hugh Mosman's will, who had done well from gold mining at Charters Towers. Archie received a 13.333 /300, which upon his death in 1918 went to Kitty. Kitty's four daughters ultimately would benefit, but it took a full sitting of the supreme court in Brisbane in 1977 to guarantee it. Once their legitimacy was authenticated, the court directed that they receive 40/330 of the fund. The benefit for Junella, May, Nora and Aprilla was $1,683.42 each. With the passing of these four sisters, uncertainty about the depth and scope of this inheritance passed into the minds and hearts and hopes of their sons and daughters. Having met with some of these family members on this matter in 1997, I sensed their need for justice which was beyond my calling to unravel.

Instead, I put in train my want for Jupiter Mosman to receive a proper account of his life, especially as it interconnected with not just one brother in the Mosman family. And I wanted to do this within the context of the Indigenous experience at Charters Towers: from its foundation to beyond Jupiter's death in 1945. There are other legacies to deal with which the book will reveal and I hope you appreciate. Enjoy!

CHAPTER ONE

GROWING UP

A young boy named Jupiter loved to play and get about Charters Towers with mates. He chased billy-goats up and over mullock heaps, and swam in Tom Mills' dam with Dave and George — sons of Tom Edwards, who was Fred Pfeiffer's gold mine manager. Another mate was Black Boy Friday. Jupiter "joined in games with these lads and generally mixed it up with them", remembered another friend, Arthur Callcott. Jupiter's exact age at this time is uncertain, although Arthur was adamant that "when I first went to Charters Towers [in 1875] I was 10 years of age within a few weeks, and Jupiter was a well-grown lad and an older boy than I." (C&C: April 1932: 71)

Jupiter grew up at play, as mining on the Charters Towers Goldfield delivered and promised more; with living conditions transforming from a life under calico or in bark humpies to cottages made from sawn timber with corrugated iron roofs. In 1875, Arthur Callcott and his family lived in a humpy on the western side of town. This was across Mosman Creek at the back of Mosman Street, the main street of Charters Towers. There were very few residences in this quarter with four that Arthur remembered: "The nearest was Mrs De Castres, about a hundred yards or so away at the foot of the slope to the rear. Next was Walter Simpson's place away to the left. Then in front of them was the Flanagan family. In front of them again was a Chinese quarter almost hidden from view by a dense cluster of castor oil trees on the bank of the creek. Further over lived the Rombergs. Down below and near the springs at the back of Mosman Street, lived Tom Moody and Bob Copper, better known as 'Copper-Rose Bob'. All lived in bark humpies, except for Mrs De Castres whose place was built up on sticks. It was the only one there about with flooring boards. All the others had earthen floors." (C&C: April 1932: 71)

THE INDIGENOUS PEOPLE

At the rear of Callcott's family humpy, some 200 "semi-civilised blacks lived in gunyahs. Every night Arthur heard the yabber of the people and the barking of their mangy dogs. Corroborees were frequently held on moonlight nights, when the beating of the nulla-nullas marked the time as the warriors went through their war dance with painted features and limbs, while gins capered about in pairs with yam sticks, one holding them in both hands above the head, while the other beat time on it with her own as they danced round singing their chant. Many people went out to see their corroborees, but they had to keep a watchful eye on the mangy mongrels. Arthur noticed the women's clothing was scant, consisting of a skirt or petticoat worn with the head and one arm through the fastening hooked up on the one shoulder and the piccanniny or child carried in a dilly bag on the back, or if it was an infant, it would be rolled up in a sheet of ti-tree bark like a roll of spiced beef and carried like a swag. Arthur said they were very backward with white man's language, and conversations were carried on in signs and broken black fellow gibberish." (TNM: 14/07/1922)

There was one thing that held no charm for the newly arrived Arthur and that was when having to pass the gunyahs to get firewood for his mother. For when the big black fellows were away foraging for tucker, the younger ones would be left to look after the camp and were always playing at throwing nulla-nullas and boomerangs, and they would not think twice about throwing one at a white boy. It was single handed. They were cheeky wretches for they knew nothing of consequences and cared less. "One friendly black boy who took a liking to me gave me a bit of advice which I respected and that was never to walk in front of a black boy in the bush, as the temptation to strike was too strong for him to hold back." Importantly, Arthur Callcott knew that while Jupiter was Indigenous, he did not live in this part of the town and hence did not belong to these people, the so-called Burdekin tribe.

BEAUDESERT STATION

After growing up on the Charters Towers Goldfield, Jupiter moved away to work with cattle on Beaudesert Station. Beaudesert was a White family partnership that originated on the upper Logan River in south-east Queensland. The family had branched their interests into North Queensland, when the youngest son, Albert William Duckett (A.W.D.) White, took up Bluff Downs on fine plateau country to the north of Charters Towers in 1872. In 1877 A.W.D., White rode west with two horses (one a pack horse) to look for more land to fatten their cattle. He was attracted to the mitchell grass plains in the central north-west of Queensland, where he formed Beaudesert Station near present day McKinlay in partnership with the Collins family, who were also from the upper Logan. (QSA: 75680, 75677) The place was managed by Walter Samuel Hickson. For a number of years, Hickson organized its stock to be walked to markets in Townsville, Sydney and later Victoria. In 1883 pastoral surveyor, nom de plumed 'Christophus' featured Hickson's organization of his workers on Beaudesert in this way:

> "What strikes one most forcibly is to see the gins, who are employed as stockmen nearly everywhere out here, strutting about in moles and flannel shirts, with felt hats crammed extinguisher fashion on their lovely heads, and smoking short black pipes. Oh woman, how varied are thy charms! They make first-rate stockmen — I beg pardon, stock-women would be more correct — and are splendid trackers. Kitty, head stockman at Beaudesert, is an adept at the latter art, and, as the saying is, could track a mosquito up a stone wall." (BC: 08/11/1883 – 3)

Going with 2,000 bullocks from Beaudesert Station near McKinlay on a long drive to Wodonga in Victoria was an occasion Jupiter took special pride in: to be part of a droving trip that took six months and five days to complete over the summer of 1889–1890 that never lost a hoof. In his final years, Jupiter recounted this droving experience to writer Jean Devanny. He told her, "I dream of the big drive I once made. Thousands of head of cattle. We got four pounds a head for the lot." (Devanny: 138)

Mosman Street Looking South, 1877 – photographer unknown – Charters Towers Archives – 2005153.1779.

CHAPTER TWO

THE DISCOVERY

Jupiter's cattle days in western Queensland coincided with the observance of the 20th anniversary of the establishment of Charters Towers in December 1871. By this time, the place had become a permanent goldfield, with continuing prospects following the opening up of the rich Day Dawn line of reef by Frederick Pfeiffer in 1879. This was followed by the opening of the railway from the coast at Townsville in 1882, the arrival of outside capital to fund deep mining and the discovery of the Brilliant Reef by Richard Craven in 1889.

Celebrations in 1891 highlighted the town's advances and recounted how the first gold was found by a party of outside prospectors. All as such was written and well-illustrated in the first Christmas Number of the newly published Northern Mining Register; the weekly paper being the precursor to today's long running North Queensland Register. By this time, it was well established that Hugh Mosman led the party that made the first discovery of gold at Charters Towers. Hugh was the eldest of 11 children, who was born at Sydney on 11 April 1843. His parents were Archibald Mosman, a pioneering whaler of Sydney who had built his station on Mosman's Bay, and Harriet (nee Farquharson). The family fell on hard times, but revived their fortunes as pioneers of Armidale and Glen Innes in the New England District. Even so, Hugh was educated at King's School, Parramatta. At age 22, Hugh Mosman moved to Queensland, where he took up Ingle Downs on the Mackenzie River in 1865. To the west was Beaufort Station, which did well in the hands of Arthur Hunter Palmer. Palmer is of some note in that he was a business associate of Hugh's father, who went on to marry one of Hugh's sisters, Cecelia. He would later become Premier of Queensland. Palmer employed John Fraser to manage his interests on Beaufort and elsewhere when he was headquartered in Brisbane. Ultimately, Hugh's grazing ventures on Ingle Downs, and later Ironbark, failed. So in 1871, he ventured north with John Fraser to look for gold. A neighbour from the Mackenzie River district, George Clarke. who had pastoral and most importantly the essential mining experience completed the then-described party.

The geologist-explorer Robert Logan Jack had written first about the gold discovery at Charters Towers in 1879, which Mining Warden Philip Sellheim reiterated in 1887. (V&P, 1887: 23; Jack: 4) And yet, the first variations in the discovery story were soon evident when a correspondent for the Queenslander wrote the following in 1886:

> "Messrs. Hugh Mosman, Samuel Fraser, and George E. Clark, were on a prospecting tour in the great granite belt in which Charters Towers is situated, and while searching in vain for water near the Seventy-mile Hill — now known as Mount Leyshon — determined to make, as good bushmen generally do for the nearest hilly country, in which stood out in strong relief the hill now known as the Towers Hill, and in the Gap, or North Australian Gorge, they found a clear stream, in the bottom of which could be seen specks of that metal which always makes the prospector's heart glad — gold." (Q: 29/05/1886 – 848)

Hugh Mosman did not write an account for the Northern Mining Register in 1891, as apparently he was on holidays, while Fraser had been dead some 17 years after venturing north to the Palmer Goldfield and succumbing to the wasting effects of dysentery in July 1874. Instead, George Clarke, then living and prospecting in the Herberton District, provided the following account to the newspaper:

> "The close of the year 1871 found Mosman, Fraser and myself in the Broughton River country, near what is now known as the Seventy Mile. Some months before, we had started from 450 miles south of Ravenswood on a prospecting expedition. We spent some weeks of fruitless searching in and around Ravenswood, which was then a promising goldfield. Then we travelled on Westward prospecting the Burdekin River country. Sometimes we got a little gold, but not what we considered payable, still we determined to keep on for a year longer if necessary. The valley of the Burdekin Westward and North-west was untried country, and somehow, being young,

comparatively inexperienced and enthusiastic, we were always sanguine of discovering a good goldfield. If not, we determined to go still further north. It was a pleasant life, and, although disappointments were numerous, yet the possibilities, if somewhat uncertain, were great.

“We prospected the Broughton branches, getting a little gold almost everywhere we tried, becoming more plentiful as we neared the Seventy Mile pinnacles, and we said to ourselves, ‘Among those hills we will get it very heavy.’ We were disappointed; we obtained nothing very good and a party of three or four men Crichton and others, whom we found working a creek, were getting very little. A considerable quantity of alluvial was afterwards won from this field, which was called the Seventy Mile, it being 70 miles from Ravenswood.

“Here we remained for several weeks, prospecting country to the south and to the West most of the time. On the top of the pinnacles, we found stone carrying gold, and on the slope of the same pinnacle, Jimmy Pill, an old Towers identity, afterwards crushed 100 oz to the ton and upwards. This, I believe, is now known as the Mount Leyshon mine.

“A cluster of conical and square topped hills away to the North had often attracted our attention, and we determined to prospect in that direction. We found gold in the locality of the Merrie Monarch lease, but not payable. From these the hills were about four or five miles distant. It was a dry time, the nearest water five miles away in an opposite direction. A storm was near, and while we were deliberating as to whether we should go to the water, or camp and trust to the water coming to us, the question was settled rather abruptly. A terrific peal of thunder started our pack horse at the best pace through the bush — an unlucky stampede, resulting in the loss of all our cooking apparatus, except one tin dish. Rain fell in a perfect torrent, and we camped at once.

“The following day we went through a gap between the hills which had so long formed the subject of our observation, and camped near the outcrop of the North Australian reef. Masses of quartz were strewn about the surface, which we at once saw were very rich, and when afterwards crushed, they yielded 3 oz and upwards to the ton. Stone raised from beneath the surface from the North Australian went 4 oz to the ton. The following day, we found payable quartz in at least half-a-dozen places—reefs afterwards known as the Mary, Wyndham, Moonstone, Ophir, Rainbow and others. In the Rainbow we got the richest specimens. We prospected for several days, finding other reefs carrying gold and we then went back and moved our permanent camp from the 70-mile to Charters Towers. There was no time for proving reefs by sinking, so after a careful examination of surface blows, we selected the North Australian. Ophir and another, the name of which I forget, as the best, and on January the second, Mosman travelled to Ravenswood and applied to Warden Charters for the reward claims.

"Then, the rush set in, and in a few weeks there were several hundreds of miners on the field. In the meantime, we had found the Washington, Old Warrior, Alexandra, St Patrick and others. The Washington was, I think about the best surface shown on the field. From this reef, from the surface alone, we took about 1600 oz of gold. The subsequent history of Charters Towers is known to all."

Hugh Mosman – Mosman Public Library.

CHAPTER THREE
SERVITUDE

Most people living on Charters Towers — including Jupiter — were acquainted with Hugh Mosman and his success. His North Australian Mine stood some metres pass Mills Dam, where he used to swim as a boy, up near the gap in Towers Hill at the top end of Mosman Street. Since 1878, Hugh's residence sat on a large parcel of sloping ground at the foot of the Day Dawn Ridge to the south of the town, marked out by a low stonewall fence. In fact, Jupiter and Hugh's lives were loosely linked, as Jupiter knew that the man who had led the big drive to Victoria in 1889, Hugh James Farquharson, was related to Hugh. Hugh James' father was a brother to Hugh Mosman's mother, Harriet. Brother and sister had migrated from Scotland in separate family parties and settled in New South Wales. But by contrast, nothing seemed to directly link Hugh Mosman to Jupiter at Charters Towers. Their differences in age, origins and background would have made such an opportunity less than practicable. Unless of course Jupiter had been employed by Hugh Mosman.

There was by custom and by necessity the need to hire servants to carry out paid menial work on the goldfield. This formed a lesser class to the better-off, with the larger timber residences often providing on-site accommodation at the rear for their domestic help to live in. Builder Ben Toll and his wife, for example, employed three servants in the 1890s. Public officials like the mining warden, the hospital matron and headmaster at Millchester all employed servants. At this base domestic level, many single girls and women were set to work as either a servant, housemaid, housekeeper, general servant, domestic or domestic servant. Many formalised these roles by entering into matrimony with many of the single men of the Charters Towers Goldfield. The Kennedy Marriage Register shows that in the first 12 years on the goldfield, 113 women out of 600 who married at Charters Towers were servants by occupation. Many of these girls and women arrived directly from England and Ireland on emigrant ships through the port of Townsville looking for better circumstance; as when in 1877, servant girls at Charters Towers were being paid 30s per week: (TNM: 17/11/1875)

> "There is a shortage of them here. As soon as a good looking one shows, she is scooped up by a miner and joins the married ranks." (TNM: 16/06/1877)

And there was a further economic sub-class of people who worked for little or no pay in lesser circumstances on pastoral holdings outside Charters Towers: "They make good shepherds, and the gins, when properly drilled and cared for, make expert and cleanly domestic servants. There are no better stockmen than the Aboriginals. They are not suited for heavy work, but there is a field for their profitable employment, in light field work, in gardening, and even in domestic service in the towns." (TNM: 21/08/1888) Such profitable employment in the town, let alone visibility on the streets and referred to individually was in fact rare. One exception was 'Jupiter the black boy', who was ensconced in a household with two well-to-do bachelors: the assayer Edward James Coane and 38-year-old John Henry Adams, manager of the Australian Joint Stock Bank who shared a house in Aland Street. The three took meals at the Royal Hotel in Mosman Street, that is until Adams lay on his bed before breakfast one morning in August 1886, put the bank's revolver into his mouth and blew his brains out.

Another Aboriginal who was also referred to by name was Aubrey the 'black boy'. He, in all probability, worked for George Aubrey, the town's ostler. And there was 'black boy' Paddy who was also known about the place. For several years, John Matthew Carroll, licensee of Tattersall's Hotel in Mosman Street, employed an aboriginal named Peter. That is, until Peter was killed by Merivale (Maryvale) Blacks in 1879 when he was about 16 years old. The murder took place at the back of the Anglican Church in upper Mosman Street. The root cause for the violence on this occasion was believed to be enmity between the Charters Towers Blacks and the Maryvale Blacks to the north. Finally, there was a black boy in charge of George Mosman's horse 'Saint' at the Royal Hotel in Mosman Street when it was stolen in 1880. (George was in partnership with Patrick Hishon when they won the jumper in a raffle.) George was Hugh Mosman's youngest brother, who arrived on the goldfield in 1878 to work as the government's mining surveyor.

Also living on Charters Towers to be close to Hugh and George was their mother, Harriet Mosman, who in 1877 lived on the east side of Mosman Creek in a two-roomed slab and iron hut. At this time, Harriet was a 56 year-old widow of independent means. Her husband Archibald Mosman had died 14 years earlier in Sydney. With the exception of her youngest daughter Alice, then aged 15, all of her 11 children were grown up. Harriet would have been amply prepared for life on Charters Towers five years after her son had discovered the first gold there. She had already spent many years as a pioneer with a large family to care for at Armidale in the 1850s. She knew about living on the edge of European civilisation and was accepting of its challenges. Perhaps 'black boy Jupiter' from Aland Street was the same black boy who had taken charge of George's Mosman's Saint seven years earlier? He was certainly an Indigenous person, but with means well above the members of so-called tribes living near and beyond the town. *See Appendix A*

George Mosman – Mosman Public Library.

CHAPTER FOUR
THE FRINGE

The formation of mining camps, and the subsequent construction of townships west of the northern sea ports of Bowen and Townsville, commenced at the Cape River in 1867. This was followed by Ravenswood on the other side of the Burdekin River in 1868 and Charters Towers in 1872. These places of hopeful European permanence helped define relations between the Indigenous people who had lived in the land for thousands of years, and European and Chinese people who were wanting to do the same. Indigenous people were wanting to benefit from what White places and people could provide, and set about living close-by, as the group of 200 living at Charters Towers in 1875 already attest to. In April 1869, 100 'Blacks' walked into the Cape River township because they were hungry. Tension rose at Ravenswood in 1872 when "when these hardly dealt with innocents — 'the Blacks' — added to the pleasure of their visit to this town by hunting and killing the sheep belonging to the butchers in town with their mangy [dogs]." (RM: 03/08/1872) Access to European material culture was a key reason for Indigenous people wanting to 'come in' to these townships. Complaints about petty thievery of white man's things, especially in the early years around the Millchester township, were not uncommon. Thomas Mowbray grumbled about a party of 'Blacks' who had camped for a considerable time in the vicinity of his residence and had to contend with petty thefts and indecent and offensive habits. (RM: 03/08/1872) Tommy was sent to the lock up for 24 hours after he stole a pair of Edward Hoare's drawers (TNM: 24/10/1876) In the follow-on years, their lot would be reserved to the fringe of the town.

THE FRINGE CUT BACK

Arthur Callcott has already recounted the presence of an Indigenous group of people living on the west side of Charters Towers township beyond Mosman Creek in 1875. Around the same time, other Indigenous people were living near the St Patrick line of reef, at Queenton and Millchester. Here there was some economic exchange and interdependency, for example the supplying of bark for building humpies in return for tobacco and tucker. These transactions eventually wound up, as the town turned to the use of milled timber and iron roofs to construct houses. The town fringe soon pushed out beyond Mosman Street as the European population grew, resulting in the Indigenous people on the goldfield becoming less visible. And yet there were no walls or lines of demarcation to impede ongoing exchanges. Such was the case in 1883, when nine year-old Robert Hammond shot and wounded an Indigenous woman named Jenny after she approached his parent's home at the town end of Marion Street.

> "... the 'gins' were about the place and had given them some annoyance and would not go away; the boy had brought out the gun: he did not know it was loaded at the time he fired it." (TNM: 24/04/1883 – 2)

By, 1879 the nearest 'Blacks camp' to Charters Towers was three miles away. It featured when the Maryvale Blacks camped there on the Dalrymple Road before coming into town to attack and kill Peter. (TH: 13/08/1879) This place was adjacent to Buckland and Symes' slaughter yards on the north side of Charters Towers. (TNM: 30/07/1889 – 2) Here there was water in what was then called Slaughter Yard Creek, which was later named Sheep Station Creek. And here "the air [was] polluted by animal matter which contain the germs of typhoid fever. Fancy pigs rooting and eating all the offal, the accumulation of the blood and filth of a slaughter yards under a Queensland sun and close to dwelling houses." (TNM: 13/04/1889 – 3)

ALCOHOL

Most enticing for fringe dwellers was to go up town at night and take to drink. This in itself was not an unusual past time for miners on the Towers, especially with 32 hotels erected there by 1890 to frequent legally within the one square mile municipality. (TNM: 08/08/1889 – 2) But so-called European sensibilities were described as tested in late 1883 when 'Blackfellows' assembled every night at the lower end of Mosman Street that led to nightly fights. The root cause of the trouble, it was said, was a certain publican who illegally supplied them with fighting rum. Magistrate Mr Sellheim said that any man selling grog to a 'Blackfellow' did not deserve the name of a white man. (TNM: 10/11/1883) In fact, there were a number of licensees who forfeited the imperious 'white man' label, which was revealed by an undercover operation conducted by the police one year earlier.

Constables Quinn and McKay worked in concert with Cubbo Palmer to catch hoteliers in the act of selling liquor to Indigenous people. (Such an act was illegal under the law.) Cubbo was the 'plant'. He was a 'Maryborough Black' who had come from Tiaro when he was a little fellow with Mr Palmer and Mr Graham. (Edward Palmer, also known as 'Overland Ned' was the bullock driver in John McKinlay's expedition that was sent to look for Burke and Wills, who later took over the Broughton Hotel some short distance away from Charters Towers.) Over three consecutive nights, Quinn and McKay concealed their identities when visiting a number of hotels in Mosman Street and Queenton to observe or hear Cubbo ask for rum or brandy from the publican and receive it at the back door. 12 licensees appeared in court soon after. Each was fined £2 with 6s 6d costs. Gilliver was one such publican who pleaded guilty — although not all did. He said the "black came like a swell — swallow tailcoat and flash togs; I thought he was a Cingalese Chief." (TNM: 23/12/1882 – 2)

Alcohol also contributed to the deaths of a number of Indigenous men. This was usually enacted under the weight of a tomahawk, nulla nulla or sometimes with a knife, wielded by mates or enemies settling personal scores real or imagined. Indigenous man Fred Ross was killed by Willie at the Burdekin Terminus in 1882. The black tracker Toby was killed in the same year by Alligator and Mick on the southern side of Charters Towers past the Excelsior Mill. With every death being a tragic loss of human life, the number of people killed by acts of violence on the goldfield between 1872 and 1894 in European terms was not anything major: there being only 13 murders during this time as compared to other causes of death. This included 83 men who died in mining and milling accidents in the same period and 327 babies and some mothers who died from birth related causes. Lost however, was any account of Indigenous deaths, given that none of the known deaths — and for that matter, the unreported and what became of the bodies of the victims — was ever documented officially. Here was a further case of invisibility and denial on the fringe.

CHAPTER FIVE
WILLIAM MARK

In December 1882, mine manager Mr Baurele was surrounded by a mob of 'drunken Blacks' one street back from Mosman Street. "They seized him and hustled him. One of them said: 'Bale [?] you whitefellow belong this country, we drive you all out, Marks [sic] kill my brother, I kill you.' They had nulla nullas in their hands." (TNM: 05/12/1882) The person referenced in the altercation was William Mark who was the long-standing publican at Dalrymple's Great Northern Hotel. Mark had taken up the place in 1868, where he later moved to Gainsford some five miles away in 1883. (CBE: 18/04/1868; TNM: 23/07/1883 – 2) Mark was also a pastoralist who took up the Plains on adjacent ground. Hence, he was a man of some note at the first inland town of North Queensland — the tiny township situated on the left bank of the Burdekin, 25 miles north from where Charters Towers later developed. Was Baurele's ambush a case of misdirected outrage and resistance in much the same way as all of one colour or persuasion are made to be held responsible for the crimes of one? Or was the allegation true?

PASTORAL BEGINNINGS

Dalrymple, where Mark's hotel was first located, was a distant pause on the pioneering path out of the port of Bowen to the west. The township formed on the west bank of the Burdekin River in 1864, following the first take up of pastoral runs by Europeans in 1861. Pastoralists from the south arrived after the Kennedy Land District was officially opened on 1st January 1861, a little over a year after Queensland was separated from New South Wales. Here the first Queensland government set about advancing the economic prospects of a new but debt laden colony comprising of less than 25,000 people, by encouraging the take up and use of its greatest asset — land — to develop wool and cattle industries. The Act that facilitated the occupation of unoccupied crown land in the north of Queensland presumed the land was unoccupied. In fact, it was not. The Act regulated how the land was to be occupied based on what the other Australian colonies had already learnt from this experience. So here it required the squatter to explore and select his runs and then submit his applications for approval. And to discourage land speculators, the regulations included a compulsory nine-month stocking clause else the run(s) would be repossessed. (Allingham, 1978: 18-19)

The first hopeful squatter-occupants rode north from Rockhampton with the first appointed land commissioner for Kennedy, George Dalrymple, who was tasked with making a place of government at Bowen to oversee the take up of country in the new land district. After the party arrived at Port Denison to form the town of Bowen on 11 April 1861, the prospective land holders set out to find and select runs and return to Bowen before organizing their stocking from the south. The first to ride out from Bowen to inspect the country had applied for runs back in Brisbane in January and arrived at Bowen by ship. This party of 11 was headed up by former Melbourne theatre owner John Melton Black, who would take up the largest in size of pastoral runs headquartered on the Fanning River. There his party built a log hut replete with holes cut here and there for their rifles at the place they called Bella Vista. which in its current context is the former Fanning River Station. Here they knew the land was already occupied. But as party member Rowe recounted, their precautions to defend their imposition were hardly necessary: "We never saw a Black about the station for 12 months." (C&C: May 1931 – 19; Brumby: 14)

The upper Burdekin beyond Bella Vista was first surveyed and applied for by a party of six who had arrived in the north with Dalrymple: William Stenhouse, Edward Cunningham, Philip Somer, Michael Miles, and Christopher Allingham, who were accompanied by an Aboriginal man named Jimmy. William Stenhouse took up Niall on the Clarke River; Allingham at Hillgrove on the Basalt River, while Somer took up Dotswood on Keelbottom Creek. These were all tributaries that flowed into the Burdekin. Edward Cunningham took up Burdekin Downs on the river itself, near to where Dalrymple township was set up three years later. Returning to Bowen in June 1861, the party "gave a favourable account of the country, but represent the natives as very numerous and daring." (C (R): 02/09/1861) This was documented by Edward Cunningham, when he recounted many years later the journey his brother had made in 1861. When crossing the Leichhardt Range, he wrote, "a number of fierce looking savage warriors armed with spears, boomerangs, waddies and long wooden swords and painted in a most fantastic manner, running the tracks of the horses coming into the camp the evening before and evidently bent on attacking the wanderers." (Cunningham: 4) Cunningham wrote the hostility was unprovoked, resulting in his brother being wounded by a spear and Somer being clubbed. The party moved on without further contact taking place: "They came on the track of another party of explorers in the Valley of the Burdekin but did not fall in with them." (Cunningham: 4) This was Daniel Cudmore's party of four from South Australia that surveyed runs on the upper Clarke River above Niall where Tara Station was formed.

1862

In April 1862 the overland route between Port Denison (Bowen) and Rockhampton was reported to be lined with stock proceeding to the Kennedy. These herds arrived for the squatters to occupy their runs within nine months of the date of their licence. (BC: 14/04/1862 – 3) Concurrent to these events was the signing of a memorial on 14 May 1862 by squatters, stockholders and residents from across the Kennedy to George Dalrymple at Bowen. It was written "to prevent possible scenes of bloodshed which must result from a continuance of the unprotected state of the district", especially now that they and their animals were about to take up the land from the Indigenous people permanently. The signatories were representative of pastoralists and others whose take-up of the land they thought might be challenged. But it reflected their moral and civic belief that upholding law and order was best left in the hands of a police force, rather than themselves being forced into acts and receipts of blood shedding should confrontations arise. It was especially pertinent, as they were at the forefront of the take over of country owned and occupied by Indigenous people.

And yet, the first inroads into the upper Burdekin in 1861 and 1862 were being received by the original landowners in disparate ways, even with the memorial making no specific reference to deaths, let alone wholesale blood shedding having taken place at least from a European perspective. The European solution to deal with what they described as extreme hostility towards themselves was to increase the presence of the Native Police throughout the district. Dalrymple agreed with this view and recommended detachments of police be stationed in the lower and upper Burdekin and along the coast to protect the stations "from a numerous and hostile race of Aboriginals." (QSA: PR846759) This included a detachment of nine native police being stationed in the upper Burdekin to protect the likes of the Christopher Allingham from Hillgrove, the Cunningham brothers from Burdekin Downs and William Stenhouse from Niall, who were among those who signed the memorial.

And yet, the country was quiet, even with the second swipe of Europeans riding north from Rockhampton to take up the rest of the runs on the western side of the upper Burdekin in February 1862. On their way to the Clarke River in 1862, this party of four had but one encounter with the Indigenous people: when "Mr James saw a black fellow at night". (Hann Family Diary: 10/04/1862) This was much reminiscent of what had happened to Leichhardt's party while travelling up the same part of the Burdekin River in 1845. This 1862 party included William Hann, along with his brother John, who took up Maryvale, the Bluff or Bluff Downs and Lolworth on behalf of their father, Joseph. This ocurred with the active backing of geologist Richard Daintree who would reside at Maryvale, and sleeping partners back in Melbourne. James Anning was another member of this surveying party. He was one of six brothers from Victoria who all took up a vast spread of country on the other side of the range in the upper Flinders River in the Burke District centred on Reedy Springs. The final member of the Hann party was Moses Angel James who took up Nulla Nulla, which he soon relinquished to set up a public house there in 1866 — it being of good repute because it "surpassed all other North Queensland bush public houses". (CBE: 10/08/1867; QGG, 1865: 855)

James' public house went on to ease the journey out of the Burdekin into Flinders country from Bowen, when in 1864 travellers could rest at Frederick Hamilton's public house beside the lower Burdekin River, Richard Wills' house on the Haughton River and at Genge's Great Northern Hotel on the upper Burdekin River crossing. This was where the township of

Dalrymple — North Queensland's first inland town — was established that year. (Brumby: 52-53) And it was there where the request made in 1862 for police protection in the upper Burdekin was finally put into permanent effect. This happened six years later, when the district headquarters were shifted to here from Bowen, and a police barrack was erected on the left bank. (QSA 846847 - 1869) By then, police work concentrated on escorting gold from the Cape River Goldfield to Townsville. (Beforehand, occasional patrols out of Bowen had taken place, for example when William Hann noted in May 1863 that the "black police came to Bluff Downs". (HFD: 12/05/1863))

The country closed in further after 1864, when the Dalrymple township became the terminus of a fortnightly mail service from Bowen. A monthly mail service then commenced from Townsville to there in 1865, before passing through the main stations in the upper Burdekin to Burketown in the Gulf. Beyond Dalrymple, the mailman rode on to Reedy Lake, Robert Stewart's Southwick, James' Public House, Cargoon — which Richard Anning would later take up — and then over the Great Dividing Range into the Flinders and beyond. A similar service soon went into the eastern end of the upper Gulf via Hillgrove, Bluff Downs, Mary Vale, Tara, Wando Vale, Sanders Craigie and again over the Great Dividing Range and beyond.

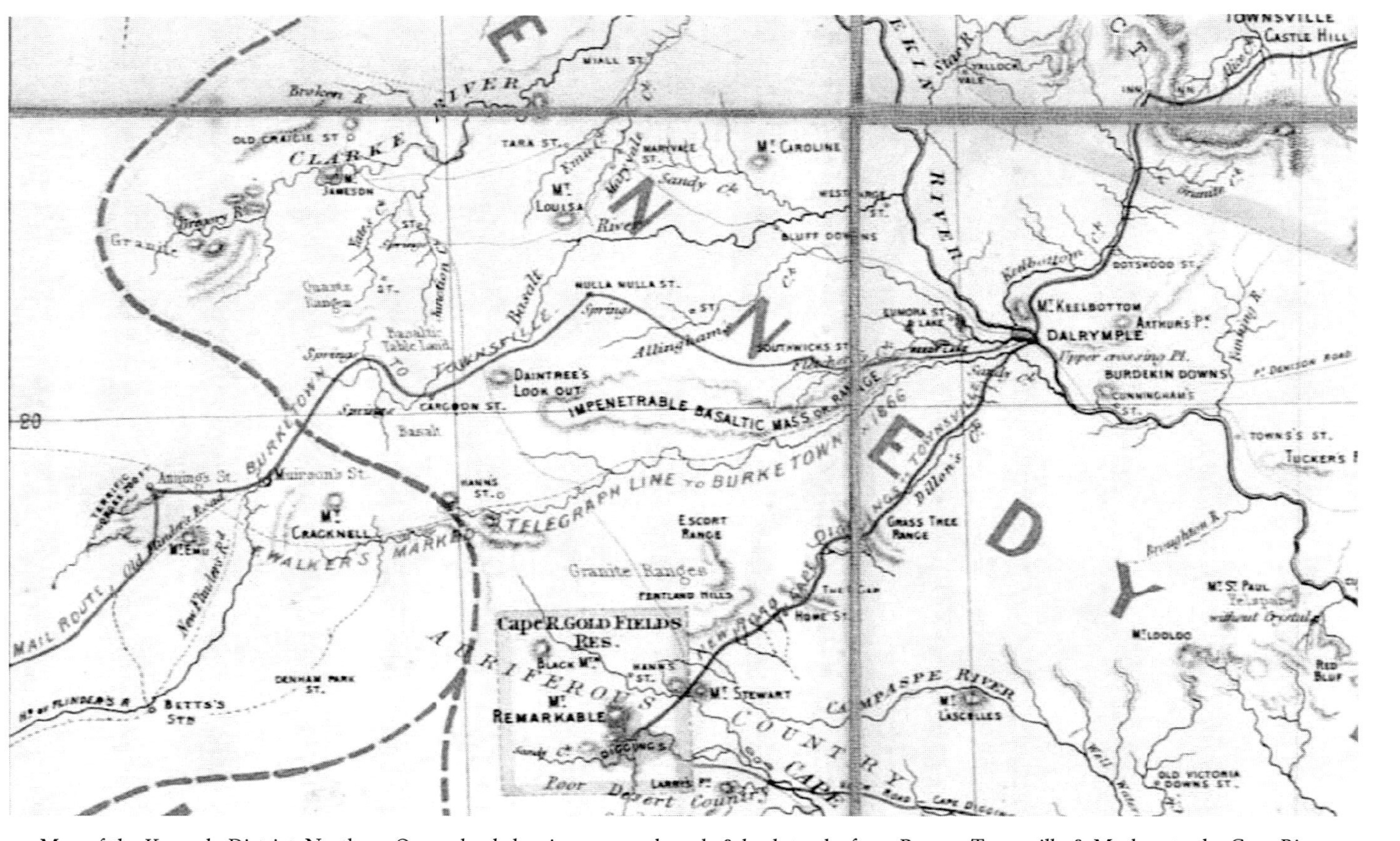

Map of the Kennedy District, Northern Queensland shewing surveyed roads & bush tracks from Bowen, Townsville & Mackay, to the Cape River Goldfields, 1868 – Charters Towers Archives – 1351.

CHAPTER SIX

THE PASTORALISTS

Letters written by one of the subsequent owners of Nulla Nulla Station, George Cain, to his family in Melbourne between 1866 and 1868, evidenced a hard life raising sheep together with a hardened regard for Indigenous people living on his runs: "N**rs been showing up; frightened a shepherd in from his sheep at one o'clock in the morning last week. Guess there's some of them that won't frighten any more shepherds. Yah! A charge of big shot that I shoot turkeys with will scatter 50 of them; only when they turn & show spears you must give 'em pepper." (Dalton: 4) W.R.O. Hill wrote in a similar vein about his time managing nearby Reedy Lake Station between 1865 and 1866. While he recounted it being a "beautifully situated place on an immense lagoon", Hill recalled a rough bush life replete with fever and blight and the constant danger from the blacks who infested "the basalt wall". Hill described this geological feature as "a peculiar formation running for miles parallel with the Fletcher and Sandy Creeks; the wall was a veritable stronghold for the Blacks, who, realising the security it was, were very bold and daring."(Hill: 31) During Hill's time, one shepherd and a number of sheep were lost. For Hill, life on Reedy Springs was never safe:

> "The wise thing to do on seeing a black was to shoot and shoot straight, otherwise they would certainly shoot you. I had several narrow escapes." (Hill: 31)

Between Reedy or Reeves Lake and Nulla Nulla, Robert Stewart had taken up Southwick in 1863. His homestead sat adjacent to the great basalt wall, 70 miles long with a mean width of five miles, averaging 20 feet in height. In the most parts, it was inaccessible to cattle, sheep and horse. And yet it bounded in water from two perennial creeks, and was abundant with wildlife. (Q: 02/11/1895 – 838) On her first ride west to

Hughenden Station in 1868, Lucy Gray camped at Southwick and recorded her impressions:

> "In this part of the country the blacks have been troublesome and dangerous, the Wall being a city of refuge to which they would always escape after they had committed depredations among the flocks and herds, besides killing white people, shepherds and whenever they had an opportunity. It was open warfare.... They were 20 to 1 with the white settlers, but their dread of fire arms left them at a disadvantage. Their own weapons are formidable when they have a chance of using them at short distances. Although they are supposed to be so numerous, we saw no trace of them on the way." (Allingham, 2008)

The Wall and its inhabitants concerned all pastoralists living nearby: when on a journey under the Wall east from Lolworth to the Burdekin in 1863, Bill Hann noticed a great number of Indigenous people there. And yet he moved on without repercussion. Unlike Hill, Gray and Cain, the Hann family barely noted their connection and engagement with the People while working on their stations. The following entries from their extensive set of diaries attest to very few moments when conflict took place. In 1864, Bill Hann went missing all day while looking for horses. This had "Mrs Hann thinking the Blacks had me". (HFD: 19/07/1864) Less than a week later, the Hann's stores were "destroyed by the blacks at the Burdekin". (HFD: 23/07/1864) In 1870, "Alfred Foote and I went to Furnish's Hut on Spring Creek. We saw that the blacks had taken all his things, also his blankets". (HFD: 10/01/1870) Such tensions and engagements were deemed part and parcel of trying to establish a place of living to work sheep without it being framed in hostility, undue fear and force of blood.

Most revealing is how the Hanns went about forming relationships with the first People through work. The Hann diaries make it clear that the use of young Indigenous men and young Indigenous boys by themselves and others was prosaic. Bill Hann refers to Toby the black boy; of drawing posts for the kitchen accompanied by a black boy; and neighbours like the Allinghams and Richard Anning being accompanied by black boys. (HFD: 17/08/1864; 22/08/1864; 26/11/1870)

The nature of their acquisition was tellingly revealed by Hann in 1870 when "Gray, Cudmore, Gardner, Shields and Finlater and self went to the black's camp at Cape Marlow [Cape Pallarenda at Townsville]. I got a little girl for Mrs Hann." (HFD: 15/01/1870) Such an act seemed to be a free-for-all for pastoralists to take their pick of either young girls, boys or young men to take back to their station and put to work. That Kitty and Topsy bolted two weeks later and that even if Kitty after being found in the bush "was quite willing to return" bespoke of even darker forces at play. In 1864, Hann knew three blacks "had run away from F. Jardine [whilst on his way to the tip of Cape York] and that Jardine's men came for them. They came to the station and secured them." (HFD: 14/09/1864) From around 1865, Frank Hann, the youngest of the Hann brothers managed Lolworth at the western end of the Great Basalt Wall. His record of dealings with the Indigenous people are the most confronting. After he had come across a steer with 12 spears in him in May 1874, for example, Frank tracked down where the attackers had gone and found their camp two days later.

> "Saw where the Blacks had camped that night. We had dinner. Went on their track and found them in the gorge. Give them a great dressing took 14 tomahawks. Took Spider the black boy. [The following day] we burnt their things. We went on their tracks. Tracked them on the head of the Campaspie. We saw them in the gorge but too late to touch them. We camped about a mile from their camp. We heard them. Wet night." (Frank Hann's Lolworth Diaries: 02/06/1874)

KANAKAS

After 1869, station activity on the Burdekin changed after the sheep industry failed in the Kennedy. This was brought about by markets being too distant, grasses and weather ill-suited, and animal management too labour intensive and dangerous. Cattle raising brought better sales through local markets, especially after John Melton Black erected a boiling down works at Townsville in 1866, and especially when goldfields opened up nearby. Besides, the country was better suited to cattle and the need for pastoral workers was less. On Allingham's Hillgrove, herd numbers of between 3,000 and 4,000 required very few hands: "those on this place being two kanakas, one overseer and one of the brothers Allingham..." (RB: 09/09/1875 – 3) Herein lay another intersection of people: men from various Melanesian islands who were 'encouraged' by visiting Europeans through all sorts of means to leave their homes to the east of Queensland to work in various situations. The first men — known locally as Kanakas — were brought to the north to help build the port of Townsville, on behalf of Robert Towns and his partner John Melton Black in 1865. Towns' grander design to use Kanakas to cultivate cotton there quickly failed and seemingly some of these men were absorbed into working for nearby pastoralists. This included the Hanns and the Allinghams and was remembered at the time when Joseph's Hann's daughter died in 1943:

> "Kanakas [like Charlie Massa or Masso] were employed as shepherds and the Blacks of Maryvale are descended from these old-time shepherds. The kanakas took wives from the aborigines and their descendants are intelligent, active, useful people." (TNM: 03/03/1943 – 6)

Charlie Santo would enter this mix after Richard Daintree departed to take up a government appointment in 1870, and W.D. (William Duckett) White and Sons purchased Bluff Downs in 1872. (Q: 05/10/1872—5) Bluff Downs was managed by one of William White's sons, A.W.D. (Albert) White, who stocked it with cattle brought up from the family property on the Logan River. (A.W.D. White later purchased Beaudesert Station from where Jupiter's long drive commenced.) One of the stockmen who brought the first stock north was Charlie Santo, who was also known as Charles Cupid. Charlie was a "Kanaka, a black man with a white heart, also an honest and reliable servant. He came from the island of Santo when a child, and at an early age was employed by the Whites, of Beaudesert." (TNM: 11/09/1943 – 6) Charlie stayed and brought about a large family.

Travellers and pastoralists also passed through Dalrymple to the south of the Great Basalt Wall, where they followed Hann Creek to the west toward Flinders country. Further south there commenced the Campaspe River, which in a good wet flowed into the Cape River before it entered the Burdekin, well to the south of Charters Towers. Here were McClelland's sheep runs, comprising of Pentland Hills, Mount Pleasant and Allandale. In October 1864, two shepherds, one presumably Henry Willmett, were murdered by Aborigines. (RB: 27/10/1864 – 2) (In 1867, McClelland's interests were transferred to John Moore Dillon with his station known as Homestead.) Further south on the Campaspie, John Melton Black abandoned his Victoria Downs soon after two shepherds were killed there two months later. (RB: 27/10/1864 – 2; QT: 03/12/1864 – 3)

> "It is said that the hut which the murdered shepherds [on Victoria Downs] occupied had been robbed previously on three separate occasions; and perhaps a certain amount of blame is attributable to the whites for not taking steps to prevent these depredations. If they had acted with firmness, and had made the natives understand that they would not be allowed on the station, this dreadful tragedy might have been prevented." (QT: 03/12/1864 – 3)

CHAPTER SEVEN

NATAL DOWNS

South of Black's Victoria Downs was Natal Downs, comprising 200 sq mile of country along the south bank of the Cape River, some distance before it entered the Burdekin. This was a place where Jupiter lived after 1900. Natal Downs was first taken up in 1862 by Robert Kellett to graze sheep and cattle. Kellett's sleeping partner was his cousin, the Irish born squatter Thomas De Lacy Moffatt, who was then the Colonial Treasurer of Queensland. Sydney merchants Parbury and Lamb, and later Parbury and Parbury, superseded Moffatt as backers after Moffatt died in 1864, with this new partnership dissolving in 1866. This was when Kellett was replaced by James Spry, a nephew of one of the then partners, Alfred Lamb. (QGG,1862 – 489; QGG,1866 – 622)

These were trying times for Kellett and for Spry, especially when four of their shepherds were killed by Aborigines in two separate incidents in early 1865. (QSA 846794) The trouble was so serious that Kellett wrote to the Colonial Secretary about his concerns: indicating that he was prepared to build a police barracks on Natal Downs to quell the trouble. After all, he argued, the station at that time was on the main road from the port of Bowen to the Flinders. Even so, barracks were not built on Natal Downs, because a police camp was already planned for Genge's [Dalrymple] further upstream on the Burdekin River. This took place in 1868, which was coincidental to William Mark taking over Genge's Hotel there on the right bank of the river.

In the meantime, the Native Police continued with their visits to Natal Downs and other runs from out of Bowen but with no resultant down-turn in attacks and violence; in July 1866, James Kelly was killed on the Far Cape. "Mr Spry, and a party of whites went after the blacks but of course found, as they expected, the man Kelly dead." (SMH: 14/08/1866 – 5) Lt Murray of the Native Police turned up on the 21st when it was reported that "he paid a great attention to the poor blacks in the way of dressing them." (SMH: 14/08/1866 – 5) Further trouble was experienced in 1867, when for the second time, the shepherd Christian Ivors was wounded and "much ill-treated by the Blackfellows". (BC: 23/03/1867 – 5)

WILLIAM CHATFIELD

26-year-old William Chatfield, a grandson of the then prime backer from Sydney, John Lamb, took over as overseer on Natal Downs in 1868. (Chatfield was later an owner in partnership with Charles Parbury, a son of John Lamb then based in Brisbane, and Michael Miles until 1873. Chatfield subsequently owned Natal Downs on his own account.) He brought about a change with respect to how Indigenous people were to be treated in the future on his runs.

> "Until 1868, the Native Police used to visit this station constantly. The result was shepherds killed, and sheep, cattle, and other property destroyed to the value of £200 a year. At my request, in that year the Native Police promised to visit me as little as possible and not interfere with my blacks (which promise had been kept by the various gentlemen in command in the district since); with the result that I was able to explain to the ... that if they kept away from the cattle camps and did not molest the shepherds they might hunt and camp all over the run." (Q: 10/07/1880 – 50)

Chatfield had arrived in North Queensland from Sydney in 1862 and had worked in the area since 1864. He was on Natal Downs when the troubles with the Indigenous people brewed in early 1865 when he provided a statement — he, knowing about the damage done, and he too knowing its cause. But once he was in charge of the station, Chatfield allowed the Murrays to come in rather than keeping their relationship at arm's length and mediated by an external agency:

> "Damage costs reduced, the Blacks became friendly and the old days of reprisals that of shooting the men and destroying their nets, water bags, and implements came to an end. Previously and without this property, the old men, women and children starved to death as they were hunted into the

spinifex (desert country). Chatfield got to know the people personally and indiscriminate punishment was avoided. The tribes to whom this country actually belongs are only too glad to act as police and give up offenders." (Q: 10/07/1880 – 50)

The success of Chatfield's letting-in strategy became known in the district and was noted by the likes of Hifling and Peterson, Thornton & Co, and McDougall. All were keen to adopt a better means for land owner and land holder to live together amicably rather than with enmity. (BC: 06/02/1869 – 5) Chatfield engaged in a significant discourse with the Indigenous people for nearly 13 years, whereby he sat down with the People to learn about their culture. For example, he was taken to two quarries to the north of Natal Downs, where they chipped stone into tomahawk heads. This was a remarkable experience given such quarries were not that well known about. Chatfield also received instruction into their language and recorded a sizeable vocabulary of the Yuckaburra dialect. He conveyed their words to the Royal Anthropological Institute in London in 1872 and these were published in their journal in 1874. This formed part of Edward M. Curr's The Australian Race: Its Origin, Languages, Customs, a four-volume continental survey of Aboriginal peoples.

DECLINING NUMBERS

A working relationship between Black and White based on mutual respect and mutual interest resulted in Chatfield voicing full praise for his new workers on Natal Downs: "At the present moment I have six blacks lambing in charge of an overseer, and two boys shepherding, and for all these purposes find them quite equal to, and as careful as white men." (Q: 27/06/1874 – 5) Like many observers of Indigenous people at this time, Chatfield expressed the dominant view that "there is little doubt that the doom of the race is utter extermination within the next 50 years; whenever brought in contact with Europeans." (Q: 27/06/1874 – 5) He certainly knew about declining numbers in the district being largely brought about by disease: "[In 1870] the Yuckabuura could muster 130 fighting men. Now it could not muster more than 40 at most and few children are growing up. Measles in '65 and the vices of civilisation since have caused this rapid decrease." (Q: 10/07/1880 – 50) The losses were so bad in 1875 that it was reported "there are not enough left to bury their dead. This may be an exaggeration but it is generally known that the natives over a large extent of country are suffering from this disease..." (DNA: 21/07/1875 – 2) The impact on Natal Downs and further south on the Belyando and Suttor Rivers created a great havoc with the 'Blacks' being decimated very fast. (RB: 14/10/1875 – 2)

William Chatfield settled well into his new country. He had brought a Sydney bride north in 1871 and they raised a family of three surviving daughters. All settled into pastoral work and living on Natal Downs for the next decade. Travellers passed through the run above the Cape when making their way from Bowen to the western downs country along the Flinders River. This shorter route was trialled after gold was discovered in the upper Cape in 1867. But John Melton Black's Townsville quickly won out as the entrepot to the Cape, by virtue of it being of a lesser travelling distance. Hence, the Cape River route fell out of favour when a track was pushed west from Dalrymple along Dillion's Creek via Dillon's Homestead Station to the Cape River Goldfield.

Chatfield adjusted his commercial interests away from sheep after gold was discovered at Charters Towers in December 1871. A droving route was eventually pushed through the bush to take cattle to the growing butchering market where he opened a shop there in 1877. (TNM: 24/03/1877 – 3) Owner-editor of The Northern Miner, Thadeus O'Kane, took some delight when announcing the 'Kanaka man' was closing the business in 1879. His prejudice was deliberate and thin skinned and typical of O'Kane, especially given Chatfield's standing in the Charters Towers community — being a life governor on the Charters Towers Hospital and elected to the first Dalrymple Divisional Board in 1880. William Chatfield died in Sydney from ill health in 1881 aged 39 having been, until this time, one of the oldest residents of the district. (BC: 17/09/1881 – 6)

CHAPTER EIGHT
DALRYMPLE TOWNSHIP

Before the formation of Charters Towers in 1872, the township of Dalrymple was the key transport hub for pastoralists and their northern stations in the upper Burdekin. It was the first and last place on the roads west and north where provisions and necessities could be purchased: "Station hands from the Flinders and elsewhere, stock drovers coming down after delivering cattle, diggers from the Cape River, Etheridge, and Palmer, all meet here, and being the first place where grog can be obtained, there are very often some rather rough 'sprees' generally ending in a good free fight." (RB: 18/06/1875 – 2) But three years later, it presented as a sleepy hollow of 50 people, with one main street built only on one side where there were two hotels, two stores, a saddler's, a blacksmith's shop and a post office. The sole policeman was resident on the opposite bank to the township where a detachment of native police had been headquartered until 1874. (MMSKA: 14/02/1874 – 2) The then nearest police camps were at Charters Towers and Millchester.

A track and telegraph line from Dalrymple to the south was only pushed through after Charters Towers had come into being. Until then, Europeans had not spent time on this open plain broken by gullies and occasional hills. Leichhardt in 1845 and later Gregory's party in 1855 had stuck close to the Burdekin River to the east and missed this locality. While Charters Towers grew up close to the western boundaries of two pastoral runs named Texas and Oregon, they were never officially occupied by the first applicant William Hodgson in 1861 or his successors, John Melton Black and Robert Towns. Hence, the country was never made known to run owners and their workers, as the country's value to grazing animals was testy: "The soil in the neighbourhood, while fertile enough, was not particularly rich in pasture, although when the climatic conditions are congenial, the growth of vegetation is remarkable. Ironbark and other trees grew over the site of the town." (TNM: 09/10/1899 – 3) Opportunistically, brothers Michael Wickham Cunningham and Edward (Ted) Cunningham from Burdekin Downs from the opposite side of the river, steeled some advantage from these empty runs and adjacent country after building a cattle camp on the lower part of Mosman Creek, near present day Lissner Park, and putting it to some use in better seasons. (Gray – 150)

With the township of Charters Towers in place, tracks fanned in from the north from Dalrymple and beyond; east from the Ravenswood Goldfield and west in a more direct line to the Cape River diggings and beyond. Most important of all was the setting up of a transport corridor to and from Townsville on the coast through Reid's Gap, beginning with a road crossing the Burdekin at Fred Hamilton's Fanning Downs. By the time Billy Mark was roughed up in the back streets in 1882, Charters Towers starred as a centre for mining and business activity in all directions for some distance, which was enhanced when the railway opened from Townsville in December 1882. This paralleled the existing rough road from the coast. (TNM: 8/6/1901)

BLANKET DAY

The tracks into Charters Towers stimulated commerce and social engagement from well beyond the town boundary. This included Indigenous people from both sides of the Burdekin River, those who clustered on various district's pastoral lands and those on the town fringe. And yet, there was only one official occasion when Indigenous people could use these paths to make their way freely into the very heart of the goldfield. This was when they could each receive a pair of government blankets for protection in the soon-to-arrive cooler months of the year.

The annual distribution of blankets to Aborigines was a well-established practice at towns throughout Queensland with noted Indigenous populations. The custom served to mark the birthday of Queen Victoria, which was on 24th May. The distribution at Charters Towers, however, was held on the 1st May and organized through the office of the police magistrate at the back of the courthouse in Gill Street. Magistrate Sellheim conducted the first recorded proceedings in 1882, when it was described as the normal annual distribution. On this occasion, 180 blankets were given out. This was followed up the following day when another 39 were given to the 'Blacks from the Burdekin'.

> "The blankets are of a very fair quality, and it is a pity the government don't put a mark on them by which they can be distinguished as a great many blacks dispose of them to unprincipled persons for a fig of tobacco or a glass of grog. After all had got their blankets, they stood up, took off their hats—all those who had any—and gave three cheers for the Queen."

Photographer Arthur Bailey captured the distribution of 1889 when it took place in front of the new Court House in Hodgkinson Street. Here, a large crowd gathered to watch proceedings:

> "The blacks began to muster about half-past 10 and by noon when the proceedings commenced, there were present 76 men and 71 women and 21 children, in all 168, being six less than attended on the 1st May 1888. They were for the most part decently attired, especially some of the girls who had evidently come from stations where they had been living in service, but in many instances their garb was of a decidedly eccentric nature, one old chap causing considerable amusement by appearing in an old belltopper, but about four sizes too big for him. They all looked well fed and happy. As soon as each one had received his blanket the whole lot formed into a group and photographed by Mr. Bailey, of Messrs. Allom and Bailey.
>
> "They then gave three cheers for the Queen, and dispersed evidently delighted with their new acquisitions. Afterwards a supply of bread was served out to each one, the cost of which was defrayed by private subscription. Sub-inspector Meldrum states that blankets will be forwarded to Rishton and the Broughton, and that several more blacks may be expected to come in within a fortnight or so. The blankets this year are grey, and of good quality, and in order to deter unscrupulous persons from purchasing them from their proper owners they are all marked with the letters Q.G. and a broad-arrow which is interwoven in the material." (TNM: 02/05/1889 – 3)

Spectacle aside, there formed an awareness of a slow decline in recipient numbers. While 219 people received blankets in 1882, only 168 received same in 1889. The annual distribution in 1901 resulted in only 45 blankets being handed out with 35 the next year.

Blanket Day, Charters Towers Court House, 1889 – Arthur Bailey photographer – Charters Towers Archives – 25014.

CHAPTER NINE
THE ACCIDENT

Jupiter was never part of the town fringe and so never lined up for a government blanket. This was because he had been able to attach himself to the inner workings of the goldfield through his play, his work and his sport. He was good enough at cricket, being noted as a smart fielder, to play for the Towers against a Ravenswood team in 1886. As well, Jupiter was a member of a Towers team that played football against Millchester. The Towers kicked three goals and four behinds, including one kicked by Jupiter against four behinds scored by Millchester. Jupiter was also a runner. He featured in a list of prize winners connected with the Charters Towers Athletic Club. And there was Jupiter's situation: when intimated that he was the black boy in the employ of government mining surveyor George Mosman; and later "Jupiter the black boy" when bank manager Adams took his own life. Jupiter's accommodation at Charters Towers was seemingly in good order with no concerns for how cold he might become in winter.

Jupiter's suppositive relationship with George Mosman severed after George resigned his position as government surveyor in June 1882 and left Charters Towers the following year. (TNM: 01/07/1882 – 2) As his brother Hugh explained: "George is still here ... not working ... he has been talking of leaving for sometime past, but still hangs on for some reason incomprehensible to me." (Sir Thomas McIllwraith/ Palmer Papers) Severed earlier in 1882 was the left forearm of Hugh Mosman, brought about by a dynamite accident at the junction of the Broughton and Burdekin Rivers in February. This set a low point for the northern family of Mosmans, after a hiatus was reached only months earlier when Hugh drove the pony carriage carrying his sister Harriet Ann into Charters Towers in November 1881. She was accompanying her husband, Sir Thomas McIllwraith, premier of Queensland on his first official visit to the town, where they were warmly welcomed. The following day, Hugh and George joined their sister and the

Premier when they visited the State School, where Harriet presented 400 packets of lollies to the scholars. (C (R): 03/12/1881 – 15)

George Mosman eventually left Charters Towers, while Hugh persisted with mining with continued success. This had commenced after his prospecting party discovered the first gold in December 1871. His North Australian Prospecting Claim was the first to be laid off by Gold Commissioner W.S.E.M. Charters continued to produce gold as it worked the reef on the northern side of Towers Hill. Mosman later took up two claims, adjoining the North Australian Prospecting Claim (PC) and the Eastward Ho behind the Day Dawn line of reef in 1873. He later took up claims on the Columbia and Mystery lines of reef, on the northern side of the goldfield. But all was not always smooth in returns. In 1883 Hugh conveyed to his brother-in-law's brother, Henry Wyndham Palmer, that "mining is dull at present with mundic in the North Australian...in Eastward Ho ... I may in time strike something better." (Sir Thomas McIllwraith/ Palmer Papers)

Hugh's wounding following his failure to throw a lithofracteur into the water in time while fishing was dreadful enough. It left his hand shattered, some fingers completely blown off and his wrist bone laid bare. And still, he was compelled to swim back across the Burdekin to get help from his friends, who drove him 12 miles into town where Drs. Maxton and De Vis amputated his arm between the wrist and elbow. The operation was far from successful. When writing from Melbourne one year after the operation on 24th April 1883, Hugh informed Henry Wyndham Palmer that he needed a fresh amputation: "This continuous purgatory is too much. ... It takes a certain amount of moral courage to suffer it, this I think I have and if I can get rid of the physical pain will be glad to suffer such." Hugh was about to sail from there to England for this new operation and his mother and youngest sister Alice were to accompany him: "The Mater and Alice go with me. I feel rather mean since losing my hand. The mines are looking middling. All hands are well in Brisbane. Arthur Hunter Palmer and many others are awfully kind. Seems to me more pity than kindship." (Thomas McIllwraith/ Palmer Papers) Unfortunately, it was on this trip that Hugh's mother died in London on 24th August 1883, aged 62 years. Hugh returned to Charters Towers in December 1883 to eventually strike 'something better', this time in the Victoria mine. He had selected 25 acres of ground on the eastern side of Sadds Ridge at the end of 1881, where he was hoping to cut the Victoria, Caledonia and Worcester reefs. At this time, he and prominent Townsville business man, Leopold Sache, were the principal shareholders.

"He was walking about with some pegs and a tomahawk and marked off the ground in the evening. The next day he came to lay off the shaft, and whilst he and a few who drove out with him in a buggy were selecting the site for the shaft, the horse bolted back into town, buggy, tools and all. To use Mr. Holliman's words, 'I can imagine how Mr. Mosman stood and looked after the bolting horse, and scratched his head and said hmm, so much for a new set of harness, so much for a new buggy, this is bad.' However, the horse and everything was brought back safe and when Mr. Mosman saw it, he said 'There's luck in it' and they saw the result." (NMR: 13/06/1891 – 17)

Hugh commenced a straight shaft on the Victoria and he purchased the Rise and Shine Mill on Mosman Creek in December 1883, which was subsequently known as Mosman's Mill. He went on to float the mine into the Victoria Gold Mining Co. Ltd. to overcome their initial financing challenges and later raised the New Victoria G.M.C. in 1891, through which new capital was raised and new machinery installed. Crushings eventually went on to average five to seven ounces illustrating Hugh's 10 years of "gameness and perseverance that turned the Victoria into what the North Queensland Register described as the 'best little big mine on Charters Towers and probably in Australia.'" (TNM: 08/09/1932 – 2; NQR Mining History: 45) Hugh went on to spend lesser time on Charters Towers, especially after he was appointed to the Legislative Council in 1891 and took up residence in Brisbane. Until then, his public profile had been small. He was present when the Towers Pastoral Agricultural and Mining Association first formed in 1880, while he accepted the patronage of the Liedertafel when it was first organized in 1889. Most pressing was the personal suffering he experienced when he was no longer able to engage in horse riding and jumping. Still, he maintained an unbridled interest in the turf as a horse successful owner. A highlight was winning the Queensland Derby in 1902.

Hugh Mosman – *Charters Towers: The City it Was, The City it Is, the City it's Going to Be 1872—1922* – Charters Towers Archives – 200097.4253-5 Mosman.

Group of cricketers, 1890s that includes Jupiter Mosman – photographer unknown – Charters Towers Archives – 9724.6822.

CHAPTER TEN

RESERVES

For over 30 years, the so-called Blacks' camp on Sheep Station Creek served as the town's prime containment area for Indigenous people as they made their way into and out of the town. The camp supplanted a desire expressed at various times during the late 1880s and early 1890s to create reserves, with the emphasis being on confining Aboriginals inside them. The Dalrymple Divisional Board who administered the lands beyond the township disagreed with this, saying this approach would only work "unless the same was fenced and closely watched." The idea was set aside in law as well, in the first instance by Police Sub-inspector Meldrum. While acknowledging receipt of a letter directing him to cause the expulsion of blacks from the town at night, he was concerned about the legality of such action. (TNM: 02/04/1890 – 3)

> "In Victoria and New South Wales, aboriginal stations with large tracts of country attached to them have been established with satisfactory results, and it might be possible for a similar system to be adopted in Queensland. It would be a more humane proceeding than killing their dogs and hunting the poor creatures (who, after all, have a good title to live in the land) about like a lot of wild beasts." (TNM: 31/08/1889 – 3)

Title to live in their land in the form of a government reserve did take place in 1891, when approximately 110 square miles of country was set aside within the great basalt wall bounded on the north by the Bluff Downs and Southwick runs. (QGG,1891 Vol 54 – 376) Here the remote Bluff Downs Reserve was contained and naturally fenced. And while it was some distance from Charters Towers and tokenistic in temper, it strengthened connection to country rather than to town and its fringe camps. And it bolstered an ongoing importance for that place as a whole, especially as a source of labour for nearby pastoral runs. Indigenous people were worked as they and their families were accommodated and fed in varying degrees of treatment and respect, depending of course on the owner in question. Links to runs and owners became strong through work and play. In the bush all was the same but different.

PROCESSIONS OF WELCOME

Good title to live in the land made for so-called kings of country, who at this time included King Sam Graham of the Burdekin and King Billy of Dalrymple. They were presented to the Governor of Queensland Sir Henry Wylie Norman at Charters Towers in 1890. They then ran to towers built on either side of the arch at the foot of Gill Street, and mounted to the niches placed there for the purpose. "They formed a truly magnificent picture, and stood their ground still as death. So they appeared when the procession passed." (TNM: 24/04/1890 – 3) Sam and Billy formed part of a rich pageantry displayed that day at Charters Towers. Further up the street, publican Dittman flew a German national flag over his hotel, an American flag decorated the arch built further along, while a collection of Chinese residents had read aloud their greeting to the vice regal visitor at the railway station. All was different on the goldfield but not always the same, let alone equal. Even so, Aborigines continued to be included in the town's pageantry when Governors Chermside and Northcote visited in 1903 and 1907. And when Australia's third governor-general Lord Chelmsford processioned through the city's streets in 1907, a small band of aborigines were accorded the place of honor at the very front of the procession.

WORLD WAR ONE

What was to be made most evident was connection to the new nation and the world beyond: Australia during its first patriotic foray into world war in 1914, together with the epidemic at its conclusion. This resulted in an unprecedented response from workers adjacent to the Bluff Downs Reserve on Bluff Downs Station — 44 in total, along with its owner Ernest Edward Duckett (E.E.D.) White who enlisted for war service. The Indigenous workers who volunteered from there overcame the 1897 *Aboriginal Protection and Restriction of the Sale of Opium Act* that had effectively abolished their legal rights. They also steered around issues over the colour of their skin to successfully enlist for military service. The indigenous workers from the Bluff included John Huggins, Patrick Brady, Bob Roberts, Bobby Ewan and Charlie Smith: "a record of which the station may feel justly proud". (TNM: 08/10/1918 – 3) Other Indigenous men from the Charters Towers district who enlisted between 1914 and 1918 included Jingle, a police tracker, Benjamin Bridgewater, George Ryan, Jack McAllister, Jack John Brown, George Reid and Charlie Alley. Former local man William Christie signed up at Barambah, Thomas Bowen at Narrabri, NSW and Harry Doyle at Cairns.

And with the so-named Spanish Flu made more menacing by the mobilisation of troops and their close quartering in 1918, very few parts of the world were non-infected with it, killing more people than those who died in the Great World War. It arrived in Charters Towers when 15 people died with some suddenness from pneumonia in June 1919, which fell slightly to 10 deaths in July. Remembered most poignantly were the loss of additional members of the Charters Towers District in one week in August "being in excess of any one year's death rate [of Indigenous people] since [1895]." Those who 'passed over' were named as Bungie, the noted athlete; Archie Dutton the local police tracker; Harry Hayes, a stockman from Victoria Downs; Maud Savanah from Lolworth Station and Jenny George who lived near the Towers Brewery. A month earlier, Friday had died in the isolation hospital. The Church of England service was read at the grave in each case. (TNM: 18/08/1919 – 2)

One of three triumphal arches built to mark the visit of the Queensland Governor Lord Chermside to Charters Towers in 1903 – Warwick Lloyd Collection – WC 2004.211_Lord Chermside

CHAPTER ELEVEN
THE PROSPECTOR

Jupiter's life transformed in a new century in a new nation. It was marked when he was given a Europeanised identity along with a new calling. Rather than simply being referred to as Jupiter, he was named 'Jupiter Mosman' and that he was a prospector. Both pronouncements followed his discovery of wolfram at Kangaroo Hills in 1904, where he went back to guide John Roberts and F. Bicknell to confirm his find. There the party spent three weeks before taking a number of samples back to Charters Towers, which prospected well, and a syndicate formed to work the claim. (NQR: 03/10/1904-8) A year later, and again with Roberts, Jupiter Mosman discovered more wolfram, this time in the headwaters of Stockyard Creek north of Hillgrove Station. Jupiter worked with Roberts, who went on to set up a tin mine in partnership with local business men W.R. Soilleux and Fred Johnson. (TNM: 17/04/1905 – 7; NQR: 28/08/1937 – 10)

Prospecting and small-scale mining of this type often went hand-in-hand for station workers like Jupiter Mosman, who panned and scratched at every opportunity, and when time and money permitted: "his heart was always in the search for gold, for, like Mr. [George] Clarke, he had been infected with the prospecting fever. He has run over all the Peninsula fields and is credited with being the discoverer of several auriferous areas there." (TDB: 25/08/1937 – 6) This side-line occupation of station workers commenced in the north with Andrew Ross who made the first find of gold in North Queensland on John Melton Black's Fanning River station in 1862. Follow-up discoveries of gold at the Cape River Diggings in 1867 and Ravenswood in 1868 were also brought about by station workers. As to where Jupiter Mosman was employed on stations to conduct prospecting ventures is open to question, although journalist Edward George (E.G.) Barrymore named three holdings within the Charters Towers district where Jupiter worked in later life: Lolworth, Dotswood in Rourke and Munroe's time, and Wambiana. He was certainly living further south on Pat Salmon's Natal Downs between 1911 and 1918, and he certainly worked a gold show as a much older man with Crow back on Dotswood in the 1930s. (TNM: 22/07/1918 – 3; NQR:28/08/1937 – 10)

HUGH MOSMAN

What was becoming laid bare after 1901 was that Jupiter's link to the Mosman family at Charters Towers flowed through Hugh who died in 1909, rather than through his brother George — that is, when people said he was a member of Hugh Mosman's discovery party in December 1871. Some took that membership further, by stating that it was Jupiter who made the actual discovery of the first gold. This view was first tabled after Homestead resident Ted Easton, who was on the Charters Towers Goldfield in the 1870s, conversed with Jupiter Mosman on the road to the Oaks Rush in 1908. As a result of this meeting, Easton wrote a brisk letter to the editor of The Northern Miner to advocate the government grant Jupiter Mosman a small weekly allowance — say 15 shillings — to recognise him as the discoverer of the gold at Charters Towers. Easton said Jupiter was an oldish man and being "Black has not had the same chances as a white man". (TET: 15/04/1908 – 2) Five years later, a 'correspondent's' question to The Northern Miner in 1913 received this measured reply from the editor when he stated: "The aboriginal Jupiter was one of the Hon. Hugh Mosman's party when they discovered Charters Towers. He was the horse boy. Jupiter Is still in the district and is said to be a fine prospector." (TNM: 09/08/1913 – 4)

The broader truth about Jupiter's involvement in the first find was that it was being fanned out by faded informants: the men from the discovery party of 1871 who could substantiate these versions of events. John Fraser had died in 1874 and never spoke of it. George Clarke had provided his version of events in 1891 without mentioning Jupiter or even Fraser. Clarke was subsequently killed while searching for gold in New Guinea in 1895: the quintessential prospector who never lost the wanderlust. Hugh Mosman, "a quiet man not given to talking about himself", never spoke about the circumstances that transformed his life in 1871. He passed away at the family home Easton Gray in Brisbane on 15th November 1909, aged

68, leaving an estate to his relatives valued at more than £70,000. Hugh never married. Jupiter persevered with his story of the discovery, which journalist E.G. Barrymore first took up in 1918, when he used Jupiter's own account of the events of December 1871:

> "It was a dry time and on reaching the hills of his allurement Mr Mosman, seeking water, crossed at the lower portion of the upland — The Gap — and camped on the creek just in front of the old North Australian Hotel. While searching for horses in the dewy morning, Jupiter, a small aboriginal horse boy ... brought in gold bearing quartz. It was oxidised but 'colours' could be distinguished. The find looked promising and Mr Mosman took no time in riding across to Ravenswood to register his lease." (TNM: 04/07/1918 – 3)

It seemed that Jupiter's reputation and role were finally declared and being accepted — especially through Barrymore's intervention. But two years later, Jupiter learnt that Michael O'Leary's article in the Cairns Post, which was republished in the Evening Telegraph under the nom de plume 'Coyyan', reversed his progress. In that article, O'Leary stated quite generally and briefly that the discovery of Mossman [sic], Clarke and Fraser was "another instance of how men of grit will venture and succeed..." Here Coyyan failed to include Jupiter as a "man of grit" as he also failed to mention the actual means of discovery and Jupiter's role. The following day, Jupiter Mosman visited the Evening Telegraph office in Bow Street. They were happy to make the connection to him, whom they went on to describe as "an aboriginal famous for his connection with the discovery of this field":

> "Mosman and Fraser, with Jupiter came over from Clark's branch, where they were camped, George Clark [sic] coming over the following morning with the plant. Mosman, Fraser, and Jupiter camped at the North Australian and Jupiter brought in to the two white men the first payable gold found on Charters Towers, it being an alluvial slug which he picked up at the Gap, at the head of what is now known as Mosman Creek. Clark arrived the day after the find. This was at the end of 1871, and early in 1872 Charters Towers was declared a goldfield. What tremendous events were the result of that find by a simple untutored black! Next year, Jupiter says, Mr. Mosrnan sent him to school in Sydney." (TET: 10/08/1920 – 2)

SCHOOL

As to what school Jupiter was sent to in 1872 or 1873 has yet to be determined. Even so, he was back in Charters Towers when Arthur Callcott first met him in 1875. This was the year Callcott enrolled at the Charters Towers School, some four months after 200 children first turned up when it opened in October 1875, which was only a year after the first school opened on the goldfield at the nearby township of Millchester, some four kilometres to the east.

Edward George (E.D.) Barrymore, journalist – photographer unknown – Charters Towers Archives, Bassingthwaighte Collection – 2015242.5314.

CHAPTER TWELVE
CITY ACCOMMODATION

The rise in the use of motor cars and improvements to station tracks coupled to longer times set aside by station owners for rest and leisure, helped swell the city's population when property people attended winter and summer horse-racing carnivals and the annual show. Some owners and their families stayed in town residences for more than a week at a time. Others stayed with friends, while a great many lodged at the principal hotels like Collins, Crown, Exchange and Excelsior. While the city continued to serve as a half-way house for the annual distribution of blankets until it fell out of use after 1914, a greater number of Indigenous people were also coming into the city from the various stations during these annual town and country gatherings and also staying longer.

Jupiter came into the city from where he was living at Natal Downs station to attend Carnival Week in 1911. The week had been formalised the previous year when the committees of the Towers Pastoral Agricultural and Mining Association and the Towers Jockey Club agreed to conduct their annuals in the one week in July. And so, Jupiter took to the liquor booth at the showgrounds with two white mates where he asked for a long beer. This request was observed by plains-clothed policeman Detective Sergeant Odewahn. It resulted in booth licensee Joe Arscott proceeded against for selling liquor to an 'Australian Aboriginal named Jupiter Mosman'. However, the case was dismissed, as selling liquor to an Australian Aboriginal was difficult to enforce, given transactions usually took place under stealth with physical evidence hard to gather. In this case, the evidence was lacking. (TET: 15/08/1911 – 5)

After the Great War, so-called Blacks' camps on the city fringe were supplemented by Indigenous groups 'camping' at the back of some of the city's hotels. This included Bourke's Gladstone towards the bottom end of Mosman Street and the Miner's Hotel in the other direction. One hotel camper, named Lively, said he lived at the back of Bourke's for three months, while Paddy Millchester said he stayed there on a number of occasions. So too did Ralph Lang. (TNM: 14/03/1919 – 4; TET: 01/10/1919 – 3) Such 'camping' could lead to trouble. In 1920, Miner's Hotel owner Annie McGuinness was convicted £20 for each of three offences of supplying Aborigines, while barmaid Gladys Kennedy was fined £20 in default of one month's imprisonment in Stewart's Creek Gaol. (TET: 21/07/1920 – 3) The accommodation really was untenable, not just because Aborigines were not allowed to drink, but because of the risk to their health: "A worse feature is the Blacks' own carelessness about his health. They play all sorts of games in the yards of the hotels, get hot, and have a motor car ride to cool down, then at night probably camp in the yard at the hotel." The solution, according the writer was simple:

> "If the Blacks had votes we would probably see different town conditions, but so far they have not, and under present arrangements they would be far better never to be allowed to town at all. That the Blacks are well cared for outside is easily noted in the well fed appearance when they come to town, and the fine clothes they wear, which probably accounts for to some extent for the sickness among them in the town." (TET: 15/01/1919 – 4)

Jupiter dodged another drinking offence while staying at the Gladstone Hotel in 1919. Cab driver Peter Dominic Bourke had only just taken over the licence from Clifton Henry (Winks) Grant — who had only conducted the place for a little over a year after the family of war hero Hugh Quinn had held the licence since 1902. On this occasion, regular drinker Thomas McIvor, a Great War veteran, was charged with supplying Aboriginals with alcohol. Unlike Hughie Quinn for whom Quinn's Post was named, 20-year-old McIvor had survived the war. But he was not unscathed. Tom had fought for five days at Gallipoli before a bomb from a trench mortar tore away the bones and muscles from his left shoulder and arm. Tom spent time in a hospital at Malta and was repatriated home in 1916. He was compelled by necessity to work as a labourer even though he could not lift his damaged arm above his shoulder. As a family descendant accounted of his life:

> "He got about 7/6 from the government per fortnight. Alcohol was his crutch! A sad life, dying at age of 64." (Pohl: 26/11/2019)

The first of two charges against McIvor involved him supplying alcohol to Jupiter Mosman. Jupiter told the magistrate that "he always ordered horehound and lemonade and was sometimes disappointed when he got it. (Laughter.)" Without sufficient evidence, the charge was dismissed. (TET: 19/03/1919 – 2) Not so in the case of Indigenous man Ralph Lang from Mr Lyons' Wambiana Station, who admitted giving Tom one shilling to get him a drink. McIvor was fined £20. (TET: 22/03/1919 – 3)

Gladstone Hotel with Peter Bourke's horse cab outside, 1918. Peter Dominick Bourke stands on the far right with James Bernard Bourke third from right – photographer unknown – Charters Towers Archives, Veronica Balch Collection – WC 2019.4313_3.

CHAPTER THIRTEEN
CHARTERS TOWERS JUBILEE

When setting aside Carnival Week in July 1922 to celebrate 50 years of existence, Charters Towers slumbered in the shade of past glories. Mining had all but ceased, with returns in 1921 down from 205,632 oz in 1906 to a paltry 6,592 oz. For the previous 15 years, three quarters of the city's population had slowly removed themselves to securer places of employment that took Charters Towers' population from its peak of 22,059 in 1901 to a mere 5,682 in 1921. (An Australian Post Office History: Charters Towers) As people moved away so went their residences, together with many of the city's timber halls and hotels. The resultant loss and despondency were captured in 1924 by journalist and writer E.J. Brady in the following way:

> "Empty dwellings, like sardonic skulls with unlighted eyes, faced old thoroughfares which were once the arteries of a great goldfield's life. Empty offices, with the names of departed brokers, metallurgists and commission agents on their doors and corridors spoke in epitaph of souls departed." (Brady: 201)

Those from the earliest of days and who had not departed the city were invited to attend a pioneers lunch in Jubilee Week. A special table was set aside for 23 men and women who had lived on the Towers for 50 years. Jupiter Mosman was not included, even though a considerable number supported the view that Jupiter Mosman was the discoverer and hence was a pioneer of five decades standing. (TNM: 10/06/1922 – 5) Some ruled him out by saying that at the time of the discovery Jupiter was almost an infant. Former mayor, long-term resident and celebrations organizer, Fred Johnson, held this unsympathetic view. He deliberately spoke over the experience and memory of a man growing older and excluded him from the proceedings by stating that "Jupiter was not more than six and most likely about four years old: Jupiter's tribe was a Flinders River tribe. Hugh Mosman got him as a baby, and, in a measure may be said to have adopted him, but to believe the legend that a boy of four whether white or black could have done half that rumour credits him with having done, is foolish." (TNM: 14/06/1922 – 2) Aside from being excluded from the Jubilee dinner, Jupiter was not depicted with the 'men of the 70s' when they were shown off in the city's official Jubilee brochure — even though he was included with the same men in the North Queensland Register's spread. (TNM: 17/07/1922 – 2) (Joseph Holt also shared Jupiter's fate by not being included in the Jubilee booklet.)

To confute Jupiter's official omission, a childhood friend provided him with a voice and a presence in one of five potted histories of the goldfield that were published during Jubilee Week. These 'Memories' were contributed by Arthur Callcott, Jupiter's old acquaintance who recounted life on the goldfield in 1875 in its fullest. At that time, which has already been articulated, Arthur was a playmate of Jupiter's whom Arthur never forgot:

> "Returning home I was surprised to meet a black-boy, who addressed my brother by his Christian name, and struck up a friendly conversation, in the course of which my brother repeatedly called him Jupiter. He was a boy of about 14 or 15 years of age, I would judge of him then. He was certainly a few years my senior, and seemed to me quite a curiosity in the way of black boys, from his manner of speech for the times…
>
> "Yet this black boy called Jupiter could converse so fluently. Later on I became more familiarly acquainted with him; he did not belong to the Burdekin tribe, and would frequently join in games with the lads, and generally mix up with them, and in the course of conversation he would tell us all of his experiences. It was generally believed from what he told us, as far as I can remember, that he came from a station near Rockhampton, which Mosman sold out in order to come north prospecting on the gold diggings with Clarke and Fraser, and he (Jupiter) was horse boy. He often told us lads of the time how he came across the quartz stone which led up to the opening up of the field. It was on an occasion when the horses bolted with the packs during a heavy thunderstorm, and he rounded them

up on the creek through the Gap. He got down to have a drink of water when his eye caught sight of some gold in a stone as he put his head into the water, and he took the stone back to Mosman where they were camped.

"Mosman asked him if he thought he could find the place again, and he answered "Yes". The following morning, they packed up and Jupiter led them to the spot. They pitched their tent near the Moonstone, and then had a look round. They found good gold-bearing surface quartz all along the bed of the shallow creek, following it right down to the St. Patrick. I was quite surprised to read in recent issues of The Northern Miner that this Jupiter was regarded as being only an infant, or a child of four years of age, at the time of the discovery of Charters Towers. The idea is absolutely ridiculous. Who with one grain of wisdom would swallow that? Let the lads of the time who knocked about with Jupiter compare his age by their own, and you will find that they are the best judges. When Jupiter was travelling about with the party he was of an age to serve and be of use to them, not so young that he would be absolutely an encumbrance, especially in those days.

"Unfortunately no record could be expected of Jupiter's birth, but why did not those who wish to bump Jupiter out, bring the matter to an argument 25 years ago, when the 'Northern Miner' booklet was printed, instead of leaving it till now? The lads of the early days got to believe the facts of the discovery when they were fresh, and those who are left have carried the belief right through the piece and are quite prepared to hang on. Anyhow, the fact of Jupiter getting the credit of the discovery or otherwise would not alter the matter. The fact remains that the Mosman party built the Towers, and I emphatically state right here that when I first went to Charters Towers in 1875, I was ten years of age within a few weeks, and Jupiter was a well-grown lad and an older boy than I."

THE 1920s

Charters Towers and its future were portrayed in hopeful terms by freelance author-photographer Thomas John McMahon following a visit in 1925; and then by the Brisbane-based newspaper The Queenslander in 1929. McMahon said the city was entering the dawn of a new era following its decline as the state's premier goldfield. This played out slowly to 1929, as which E.J. Brady had described in The Queenslander in 1924: the journalist could still sense the city's fall from greatness. The city's population, this journalist wrote, "had leaked out some years earlier but with the leak ceasing still the ship floated — a mere hulk, perhaps a little waterlogged and a trifle unseaworthy but still a ship..." (Q: 21/02/1929 – 3) And so a building boom took place in 1929, with the prospect that electricity was to be introduced in the following year. Unfortunately, this brief rise in hope coincided with the full weight of a world economic depression being felt by the city in the follow-on decade.

Both journalists recounted the early history of the goldfield and interviewed Jupiter Mosman for their stories. McMahon supported the by-now accepted view that Jupiter was responsible for the discovery of the first gold. However, he embellished Jupiter's discovery story, claiming it had come about when "seeking a horse which had bolted, the lad became thirsty, and, while stooping to have a drink placed his hand upon a stone. He noticed the outcrop upon which he was leaning was dotted with the yellow metal for which his master was diligently seeking." (BC: 22/12/1925 – 11) The Queenslander expanded this treatment:

> "The discovery of the field was attributed to three men — the prospectors who were really instrumental in locating Charters Towers — but no mention was made of the one who picked up the first piece of richly-laden quartz and took it to the prospectors. The prospectors were the late Messrs. Hugh Mosman, Geo. Clarke, and Fraser. With them they had an aboriginal boy, one Jupiter, and it was that boy who when going for the horses, picked up the piece of quartz to which I have referred. It was at a place known as The Gap, and it was that find which undoubtedly led to the commencement of operations at Charters Towers.
>
> "As there are other records which make no mention of Jupiter's find, this might be disputed, but to me there is no doubt whatever as to its accuracy. Jupiter, who was subsequently given the name of Jupiter Mosman by his employer, Mr. Hugh Mosman, and who was also sent to Melbourne by Mr. Mosman and educated, still lives at Charters Towers. He is 65 years of age, is hale and hearty, and is probably better acquainted with the very earliest

days of The Towers than any other man could hope. I photographed him, and verified the facts which I have stated. It must be remembered, of course, that the prospectors would probably have found the field in any case. At the same time, all the old-timers I conversed with considered that 'Jupiter's' find of the first rich piece of quartz should be recorded." (Q: 21/02/1929 – 3)

Jupiter Mosman standing where he found the gold at Charters Towers, 1929 – photographer unknown – Charters Towers Archives – 200091.711.

CHAPTER FOURTEEN

UNDER THE ACT

In August 1923, Superintendent M.J. Hogan of the Cairns Ambulance Brigade invited Jupiter Mosman to go to the northern city as part of the Golden Seventies Exhibition. This ambulance fund-raising venture was planned to depict early Charters Towers as a mining town and Cairns as a seaport in order to "reproduce as far as possible the methods, customs and ideas of the good old days." (JMF) Such North Queensland days were being quickly lost as a lived experience, which the table of 23 older men and women at the previous year's pioneer dinner at Charters Towers attested to. In Jupiter's favour was that he was alive, well, and now accepted as having been with "the late Hugh Mosman and Clark at the finding of the first gold on Charters Tower". (JMF) Working against Jupiter was that he lived a restricted life because of the *Aboriginal Protection and Restriction of the Sale of Opium Act 1897*. Being 'under the Act' meant that in order to travel to Cairns, he needed permission from the protector of Aboriginals in Cairns and Charters Towers to accede to Hogan's invitation. In others words, it was not Jupiter's decision as to whether he could go or not.

Jupiter was well acquainted with the restrictive intent of 'The Act'. He knew that when he was working on stations, the Act entitled the owner to keep half of his wages. He also knew that he was getting-on and that income derived from returns from prospecting were always by chance. Easton's suggestion back in 1908 that Jupiter be given the means to secure an allowance was a big driver to setting up a framework to receive the discoverer's reward. To date, this had taken almost 15 years with no result. In 1917, Jupiter Mosman had approached local solicitor W.T. Mitchell to apply for his exemption from being under the Act to enable a freer life. While Charters Towers Police Sub Inspector Ryan opinioned that Jupiter was "an intelligent old man who has been with white people all his life", evidence from Acting Sergeant Thomas Andrews brought certain concerns to light. Andrews had known Jupiter Mosman for several years. "He is a boy who has had little schooling, can just sign his name and read print (small words only). He associates with both whites and Aboriginals. The whites with whom he associates are the ones who will obtain liquor for Aboriginals — so long as the money is forthcoming. When he comes to town for a holiday, he always brings in a quantity of cash and obtains drink through his white associates, gets into a half drunken state and when in this state becomes very impudent. When I was lock-up keeper this aboriginal was arrested and convicted for drunkenness." (JMF)

Armed with these particulars, Andrews' superior, Sub Inspector Ryan, concluded that "for Jupiter's protection I consider it is to his advantage to be left as he is." Paramount was what the Chief Protector of Aboriginals decided and wrote to Jupiter's solicitor when stating that "Jupiter Mosman, by his nationality and habits is plainly an aboriginal within the definition of section 4 of the Act of 1897 and so is not eligible for exemption under section 38 of the same act." (JMF) Drinking and drunkenness consumed a number of men and women of all sorts of backgrounds and circumstances on the goldfield. When brought before the magistrate at Charters Towers, a history of habitualness in such matters mattered to the court. That Jupiter had appeared in court twice on charges of drunkenness — in 1916 and on his own admission about 12 months previous — were sufficient indications of an Aboriginal habit to keep him under The Act, apart of course, from the colour of his skin. Perhaps Andrews thought that he was acting in Jupiter's best interests, given his perceived vulnerability when mixing with a certain sort of white person.

ALCOHOL

Andrews was well versed with wrong sorts of types since his transfer to Charters Towers as a constable in 1903 and subsequent appointment as watch-housekeeper two years later. (TET: 21/04/1914 – 2) He often gave evidence in the magistrates court in this capacity in relation to drunkenness and vagrancy offences. This included evidence against Dave, an old Cingalese who was sometimes referred to as "Jacob, a coloured coon from Ceylon". Andrews knew he was an offender of 10 years standing. In 1905, Dave was charged with supplying grog to the Aboriginals. In 1913, he was charged, convicted and sentenced to imprisonment for six months and kept at hard labour for vagrancy. Dave would eventually be found alone and dead in an old shop in Mosman Street in 1915. (TET: 23/11/1915 – 5; 29/12/1913 – 3) The locality of where Dave supplied opium in Charters Towers recounted country Arthur Callcott knew as a boy. This was where Indigenous people had been living on the west side of Charters Towers township along Mosman Creek in 1875. Their connection to this part of the goldfield had surpassed the rise of mining and its fall, even though they had not lived there permanently. The current camp was secreted between King and Stubley Streets, in the lee of Alabama Hill where remnants of the Day Dawn Block and Wyndham, once the richest mine at Charters Towers, and the adjacent Church Land Mine stood. Amongst the shafts, mullock heaps, machinery mounts and weed growth lived a small group of Indigenous people. It was an ephemeral existence for around eight to nine people, with some coming in and out of work on stations; others without capacity through age and illness who stayed longer. (TET: 14/06/1911 – 5) They endured an outdoor world in part through the give and take of Dave's dealings in grog and opium, both being banned substances. The camp was close to where opium could be also bought directly on Gard's Lane and an adjoining narrow byway behind the Commercial Hotel. Some of the Chinese living there were happy to sell the scrapings of their opium pipes they called charcoal opium. After it was mixed with water and drunk, it reportedly sent users "off their head". "When the Aboriginals from outside stations come to town, the town Blacks take them to [David] ... and trouble in the camp is sure to follow. It is difficult to get the blacks to return to their work as long as they can get the charcoal." (TET: 26/10/1907 – 1)

The Stubley Street camp was one of a number of localities being used by Indigenous people at the turn of the century. Others lay beyond the rifle range on Great Britain Road, at Sellheim, and according to the Northern Protector who visited Charters Towers in 1909, "at Sandy Creek, near Millchester, and Dalrymple Road". (Annual Report Protector, 1909 – 11) Since forming in the late 1870s, the Sheep Station Creek Camp off the Dalrymple Road continued in use and was the dominant camp for the town. In 1896, 60 to 70 people congregated there in the scrub near the creek, camping about there every year "to receive the Queen's bounty in the shape of a blanket, and take some little time to get back to their particular district."

(TET: 13/11/1901 – 2; NQR: 08/07/1896 – 21) At this time, the camp was still serving as a waiting place for the annual distribution of blankets, but with the young and old living, often staying on longer. There were occasional breakouts in violence. Regardless of complaints about the camp from neighbouring homestead holders, Queenton Shire president Robert Sayers said that "the Blacks are the owners of the country, and we cannot hunt them out of it. The police are the only persons who can interfere with them." (TET: 18/02/1903 – 3) While camping there, the young men and women in the camps were encouraged to enter into agreements to carry out casual work around the town. However:

> "The Aboriginals in the vicinity of the towns refuse in most cases now to enter into agreements which would debar them from having a spell or getting employment elsewhere when they please. The boys, particularly around Charters Towers, will only do very casual work, and make no complaints of bad treatment from their casual employers." (Annual Report, 1904)

A report of only 35 blankets being distributed at Charters Towers in 1902 seemed to indicate a saddening slide in numbers counted informally at Sheep Station Creek in 1896. (TNM: 07/05/1902 – 2) Except that by the Protector's own account, 40 men, 21 women and 6 children received blankets that May. (Annual Report Protector, 1902 – 5) This was in excess of other distributions within the district at Hillgrove of 50 blankets, and Clarke River of 17; Pentland of 25 to the west and Ravenswood to the east. Here the Charters Towers fringe was evident from the end points: the pastoral holdings where many indigenous people lived and worked.

Aboriginal Camp or Humpy, 1914? – photographer unknown – Charters Towers Archives, Shirley Shaw Collection – 2013220.4899.

CHAPTER FIFTEEN
SLOWING DOWN

Charters Towers was mad for sport in all of its forms and in all seasons. All were encouraged to compete. Jupiter played his part, as the want to involve Indigenous men had been well established in the city and the bush. Black boy horse races were often a final feature at the various amateur race meetings throughout the district. At its peak, Charters Towers attracted some the best peds in the Commonwealth to compete in the Towers Hundred. A number of meetings were conducted by the Athletics Association at the showgrounds between 1903 and 1907 with some run under gaslight. Professional runner Arthur Postle, the 'Crimson Flash' who won most encounters over 100 yards and set world records, participated in many of the Gaslight Carnivals. However, he famously lost to Bob Anderson, an Aboriginal stockman from the Richmond area at the Eighth Towers Hundred in 1905. Bunjie ran in the St Patrick's Day sports in 1905. Cubbo dead-heated in an impressive man vs horse jumping event at a Patriotic Sports Day in 1918. Man and horse both cleared 5 ft 6 inches but both stumbled at the 6 ft mark. Like war, sport crossed the colour bar.

Benefit games drew good crowds when they defied the rains in 1927, 1928 and 1933. They, along with horse racing at the Towers Jockey Club every Boxing Day, cricket fixtures and sports days, added to the 'jollification and hot weather' of the summer holidays on Charters Towers. Aside from playing cricket, Aboriginal men were encouraged to compete in so-called 'black boy foot races' and other events when visiting the city for Christmas. These were first conducted after 1900 by the Australian Natives Association as part of their new year's sports day at the showgrounds. With the Towers Pastoral Agricultural and Pastoral Association taking over these meetings in 1922, followed by the Towers Cycle Club in 1936, so-called novelty events waxed and waned from year to year according to the whim of organisers and, of course, the rain.

Signs of Jupiter slowing down in old age were shown off at the Blacks vs Whites novelty cricket game in December 1928. This was a hospital benefit match played at the showgrounds, where beforehand the players processioned down Gill Street in fancy dress. Jupiter was a well-regarded player. He had captained the Blacks team the year before, while as a younger man in the 1880s he had been a useful player for the town. This time, however, his batting wits proved slow:

> "Jupiter Mosman gave one the idea that the rot would be stopped by the manner in which he faced the attack, but age has told on this old player, and with his first stroke he placed a lolly catch into the bowler's hand. He accepted the invitation to have another go, but was cleaned bowled and gave it up." (TNM: 26/12/1928 – 5)

Eight years after playing in his last novelty game of cricket in 1928, life's inevitable snuff was almost realised when Jupiter fell ill and was not expected to recover. George Foy, known by many as the St Vincent de Paul of Charters Towers on account of his charity work, sought funds for Jupiter to be given a decent burial. Thankfully, Jupiter recovered. J.W. 'Bluey' Ward, a city alderman and a member of the Townsville Harbour Board contributed to Foy's next cause. Bluey was known for his shock of red hair and strong political convictions, at first from the left of politics and later from the right. Even so, "the down-and-out and unfortunate retained his sympathy throughout his life". This time, Ward pleaded Jupiter's case to the Minister for Home Affairs that he be sent to Eventide Home at Charters Towers to see out his final years. Agreeing to do so would mean Jupiter would avoid, like many others living under the Act, being sent to Palm Island off the coast of Ingham. Ward knew that to do so, when Jupiter was reportedly aged 76, would result in a quick and an uncaring death away from country.

PALM ISLAND

Removals of People under the Act to reserves like Yarrabah near Cairns, Hull River near Tully and Barambah in the south-east were commonplace, there being over 6,200 People re-located against their will throughout Queensland between 1900 and 1939. (Babidge: 78) The inclusion of Palm

Island as a reserve after the Hull River settlement was destroyed by a cyclone in 1918, resulting in a troubled and isolated community comprising of disparate groups of people. It was badly managed and unjustly administered by Robert Curry, or by frustrated good-intenders like Dr Thomas Bancroft. So by the time Jupiter Mosman's future was being considered in 1936, Palm Island was fully burdened: having been transformed from a pleasant place of resort run by the Butler family for well-to-do northerners to holiday on, to a place for Aborigines from all over the state to be sent to indefinitely. Circumventing the prospect that Jupiter would see out his final years on Palm was that the number of removals from the Charters Towers district was low when compared to the rest of the state. (From 1919 onwards, almost all removals from Charters Towers were sent to Palm Island.) This approximated 73 men, women and children being taken from the district between 1901 and 1938, on the grounds deemed by the local protector to be 'fair' or 'reasonable' to do so. And yet only five of these removals were validated on specific grounds such as being 'destitute' as in the case of John Dallachy in 1928; Willie, better known as Tinvale Billy, who was deemed 'uncontrollable' and removed in 1934; and in two cases in 1922 when Junie and Lily Parker were removed from Cargoon Station 'for their own protection'. The rest were removed at the whim of the local protector with no specific reason given. (The sum of all removals from Charters Towers peaked in 1915 with 15, whereas in all other years the number varied between one and nine each year.)

Even with these removals, along with a slow natural decline in numbers through ageing taking place, the Aboriginal population in the Charters Towers district after 1906 kept at around the 200 persons mark. The Aboriginal War Census in October 1915 accounted for 182 men, women and children living in the Charters Towers District: "the total of all Aboriginals and half-castes with money to credit in bank or property". 77 of the 134 men Indigenous men counted at that time worked as stockmen around the Charters Towers District. Their numbers would have been spread across most cattle stations, some accompanied by wives and children. Cardigan Station to the south of Charters Towers was somewhat typical of the larger properties employing Aborigines, where four to five men were named on its pay sheets around 1915.

After the end of the Great War and the blanket years, the use of the fringe camp to live in — even semi-permanently — was in full retreat. This explains why removals to Palm Island were always small. Longer stays in better conditions like the Miner's Hotel ceased after it was destroyed by fire in 1927, while Bourke's Gladstone Hotel lost its licence and closed to the public in 1936. The question now was: where would the People stay especially during Carnival Week and over the Christmas Holiday break?

People standing in front of grass hut, Palm Island, 1925 – Charters Towers Archives, May Kugelman Collection – 9605.7787.

The roll-up for the blackboys race, inaugural Fletcher Vale Races, 1921 – Don Peiniger, photographer – Charters Towers Archives, Bassingthwaighte Collection – 2015242.5331

CHAPTER SIXTEEN
ACCOMMODATION

An accommodation problem first loomed for the city in the early years of the Great Depression: when unemployed men made their way in and of Charters Towers while looking for work. The City Council believed it had no direct responsibility to meet the accommodation needs of this transient population. After all, its first obligation was to its rate payers, many of whom struggled in poor circumstances. Yet the health needs of the city ensured they would eventually be required to act on behalf of the visiting unemployed. An answer was finally found in August 1933 after two years of dithering, when the Council designated land near the former Bonnie Dundee mine's mullock heaps as an official place for itinerants to camp and to where they set up toilets and laid on water that included two showers. Then in May 1934, the city joined the state government's Winter Relief Programme, when it made boots and blankets available to unemployed men through the court house in Hodgkinson Street. This was the same place where the annual distribution of blankets had taken place some 50 years earlier. (Wives of the men could receive vouchers for clothing and etc., from various shops in the city.)

> "See we had a hobo camp in Charters Towers. As you know coming into Charters Towers from either side you've got a ridge. And this one, Cavey's Ridge is the biggest one. During the Depression there was hell of a lot of blokes couldn't afford ... I know it myself ... you'd jump on the trains and you'd go to another town looking for work. You might get a day's work. You didn't get the dole like today. So you had to look for work. Here it was so good. The train would be that slow you'd just step off or step on. And there was a lot that went through here because the shearing sheds and that were out in the west or they were coming from the west for the meatworks or sugar. So there was a fair traffic of them. The Council built this what we

called a hobo camp. Naturally it was built with a ground floor and it was built with round posts and round timber bar for the square timber they put on to nail the roof on. All it had was a skillion roof, with a back and two end walls. The front was open. There was fireplaces with a few heap of rocks, fire bars and a piece of tank to stop the wind. And that's where they done their cooking. It was built just this of the gate on the right hand side going into the Charters Towers gold mine site. They'd get off at Cavey's Crossing and walk over and camp there for a few days and walk over to Wellington, or vice a versa. The council used to supply their water, their sanitary and their firewood." (Bob Mark, 1999)

ABORIGINAL CAMPING

In the lead up to of the loss of the Miner's Hotel in 1927 and the closure of Bourke's Gladstone Hotel in 1936, the better-known transient population to Charters Towers was still expecting to be put up somewhere in the city for the Christmas season. In 1934, the local protector set up an 'Aboriginal Camp' on a police reserve on the south-west corner of Bridge Street and Hackett Terrace. This was an area described as one of the "chief residential parts of the city". (TNM: 21/12/1934 – 2) The Protector's action quickly raised concerns with the general public and the Chamber of Commerce who implored he provide a site on the city's outskirts. This was found on the old children's hospital reserve, which was a remote location on Great Britain Road. (Until then, its use was confined to one occasion in 1913, when a smallpox outbreak led to an isolation camp hospital being set up there.) It was only in 1938 that this 15-acre reserve was set aside for the use of Aboriginal inhabitants. This took place "when about 70 natives of all ages and sex come in to spend their holidays during the months of December and January, and besides these, there are two or three families which regularly camp on the outskits of town". (QGG,1938 – 2: 830; Dpt Public Instruction No. 65585) In the meantime, the camp that was set up opposite Eventide for the holidays of 1934-35 went ahead. But it was, in the most, a failure:

"One 'boy' told a pressman yesterday that though they had been comfortable in the camp during the holidays he was not coming to town again at

> Christmas, if he and his friends "were to be treated like n***rs and shoved out near the old blokes at Eventide." (TNM: 01/01/1935 – 2)

Thanks to Bluey Ward's remonstrations, Jupiter Mosman became 'the only black inmate of Eventide Home' at Charters Towers in August 1936. This transformed him into becoming one of those 'old blokes across the road' from the 1934-5 Aboriginal Christmas camp. In doing so, Jupiter broke through a major social divide thanks to his history and his friends.

EVENTIDE

The need for a home to accommodate and care for old people at Charters Towers was first sparked by reports of the terrible conditions that some people were living in within the town. This concern was taken to the state member Bill Wellington and the Miners' Accident Association in 1923. Both successfully put their case to the Home Secretary James Stopford. It resulted in the government agreeing to building a place for the old, with a foundation stone for Eventide Home laid in February 1927, and the first inmates admitted on 19th September 1929.

By 1930, three wards and 43 cottages were being lived in on the southern section of a 30-acre site on Richmond Hill. More buildings were erected, with the grounds and gardens becoming of note. Of the 134 admitted in the first year the home opened, 113 were men (75% being single) and 21 women. At that time, most inmates suffered from extreme medical conditions: "were it not for ... Eventide, the majority of these inmates would be occupying a bed in a public hospital for a lengthy period." (TNM: 08/11/1930 – 2) Jupiter Mosman (Aboriginal), with the inmate number 36.5605 and age unknown, was one of 24 who were entered on the Eventide admission list from April to July 1936. Others included 71-year-old Charles O'Neill and 72-year-old Frederick O'Neill with three others from Charters Towers, and the rest from other parts of North Queensland. All were aged between 63 and 86. Capacity at the time was 200 with 202 on the books. Soon after, Jupiter was allocated a room in one of the men's cottages where he lived out his final years. (QSA: COL 321 - Eventide)

While living at Eventide, Jupiter was fed and clothed, but he had no spending money. Bluey Ward again wrote to the government on his behalf:

"I must confess it is a bit impertinent on me to ask you to give him 5 shillings per week, [an old age pensioner was getting this amount] but I was wondering if you could make it 3 shillings or do something to help the poor chap." Ward's request was approved with it noted as late as 1941: "This boy receives a pension of 13 shillings per month. Please advise the Superintendent to submit vouchers monthly." By this time so-called 'boy' Jupiter was around 81 years old.

Aerial View of Eventide, Charters Towers, 1971 – photographer unknown – Charters Towers Archives – 973405.

CHAPTER SEVENTEEN
ADAM MOSMAN

In 1937 Jupiter's life story was captured in considerable detail by North Queensland Register journalist E.G. Barrymore — this being an expanded version of what he had first written in 1918 about the gold discovery of 1871. Jupiter, he had written at that time, brought in gold bearing quartz while searching for horses in the dewy morning. It was oxidised but 'colours' could be distinguished. But now, two decades later, Barrymore wrote that Jupiter was "attracted by a stone, in which his microscopic eyes had seen 'colour'. Picking up the stone, he brought it to the prospectors. It was almost pure gold. It was gold. No doubt about it, and, what was more, there were tons of gold bearing brownstone quartz covering the surface." (TNM: 25/08/1937 – 6) Barrymore built-out Jupiter's beginnings, writing that he had come into Kynuna Station in Western Queensland as a small boy over 70 years ago. This was when "white men were pushing out into the west and the Blacks were coming in". Hugh Mosman, his brother Adam and Mr Fraser, he wrote, took up or owned nearby Tarbrax Station and "while on a visit to Kynuna, Mr Mosman took a fancy to the dark eyed smart little stripling, acquired him and took the boy back to Tarbrax". The boy's eyes were large, luminous, and as lipid as a planet and so he was dubbed Jupiter. As he then belonged to Hugh Mosman, that surname followed.

Herein, another member of the Mosman family was named as having spent time in North Queensland. Adam Mosman was born on 3rd April 1849 at the family home, Bank Cottage, in Armidale in northern New South Wales. While his older brother Hugh had attended King's College when the family were still living quite comfortably in Sydney, he and his younger brother William were sent to Newington College, Sydney. (Newington College: 08/12/1998/, Kings College correspondence,1994) Brother Hugh at age 22 had taken the lead in trying pastoral work in Queensland, with his ventures ultimately failing. This commenced when he took up Ingle Downs in 1865. This was on the Mackenzie River north-west of Rockhampton, adjacent to the original road from Rockhampton to the Peak Downs mining field. In between this lease being transferred in 1868, Hugh took up nearby Ironbark Station in 1867, which he forfeited in September 1869. Brother Adam followed north with similar results: he initially taking up run leases on Pine, Copperfield, Nepowe, Preston and Rienza in the Cook District in 1872. Their rents were soon unpaid, after which W. Barker purchased all five in 1877. Adam next applied for Rupert's Creek in the Burke District in 1873 but with rents unpaid, it was forfeited by the end of 1875, when it was taken over by W.C. Bundock and then by James Thompson.

> "Thompson bought his partners out and became sole owner, and as time went on, he acquired Rupert Creek from Mr. Mosman and renamed it Tarbrax in memory of his birthplace." (TDB: 24/11/1930 – 5)

In 1916, the Mosman connection to Tarbrax was then fixed into memory by Fox in his History of Queensland as fact and reiterated by Barrymore; in reality, it was Adam's brief involvement with Tarbrax, rather than Hugh's, that actually post-dated the gold find at Charters Towers in 1872. With Adam Mosman pursuing other pastoral ventures in other land districts soon afterwards, one can possibly conclude that it was Adam who had ventured to the west before 1872 and acquired Jupiter at Kynuna, and that perhaps Hugh was in Adam's company at that time and took the boy, as Barrymore stated. Little lingers of Adam's role in Jupiter's acquisition, as his life was cut short on the American west coast 10 years later. Much to his brother's consternation, Adam arrived on Charters Towers in 1883. Hugh wrote: "Adam talks of mining ... advised him to stick to something he knows something about ... his luck has been good and may stick to him in mining ... had knocked off drinking for three years. It is to be seen whether this resolution stands the test of time." (Sir Thomas McIllwraith/ Palmer Papers) But there was a change in heart. Adam acquired 640 acres of land at present day Rollingstone, north of Townsville that same year. He named it Armidale, in honour of his birthplace in New South Wales. (QGG, 1883: 1 – 762) Adam married Emily Adelaide Finch at the Day Dawn Hotel in Townsville on 10th September 1883. As to how far he and Emily were intending to travel by ship on their honeymoon is not clear. The home country would have been a draw at the time, as brother Hugh had left for London in April in the company of his mother and sister for surgery on his arm. Harriet died in London August; Hugh's stump was operated on in October and he returned to Queensland in December. But Adam Mosman died at San Francisco on 14th January 1884 from erysipelas or red skin. (TNM: 26/04/1884 – 1)

ADAM AND THE DISCOVERY PARTY

Jupiter knew Adam Mosman because as far as he recalled, Adam was a member of the Charters Towers gold discovery party in December 1871. He disclosed this in February 1939, in response to yet another recount of George Clarke's discovery story that had been first told in 1891 and was becoming well repeated. Jupiter was not impressed by Clarke's version of events and wrote so:

> "Discovery of Charters Towers. (To the Editor.) Sir, I read a story of the history of the discovery of the goldfield of Charters Towers and being, I think, one and only of the team left, I would like to correct same and give you a true account of how it was found for I think what appeared in the Townsville Bulletin is not quite right. Mr. Clarke says he started 450 miles south of Ravenswood. Now I remember we went from Townsville and Mr Clarke joined our party In Ravenswood. Our party consisted of Hugh Mosman, Adam Mosman, and Fraser, and myself, a boy. After Clarke joined us, we came on up the Seventy Mile to Clarke's branch and we left Clarke there with most of the outfit near where Mount Leyshon is now, and we went on to the hills now called Charters Towers and we used to make mounds of stone to guide Clarke as he was following on. We went on to a gap in the hills and camped. Our camp consisted of a small fly. I had been out and found a nice piece of stone and went back to inform Hugh Mosman and he brought a pick and we dug it out, and I can assure you that is what started the mine called the North Australian. Jupiter Mosman, Charters Towers" (TDB: 20/02/1939 – 10

Adam Mosman – Mosman Public Library

CHAPTER EIGHTEEN
THE SPIRIT OF FREEDOM

While living out his final nine years at Eventide, old man Jupiter Mosman came of age. He was conferred respect and received acknowledgement from the most influential for what he had effected as a child in 1871. Jupiter found his voice when his own story was finally heard in 1939, even if future re-tellers would more often than not revert to George Clarke's misinformed account of the discovery. Jupiter also received a material reward that was forged — again by chance — through his friendship with taxi driver Bill Bourke. For a number of years, he and Bill had got into the habit of buying shilling half-share tickets in the Golden Casket. In March 1940, they and five other Charters Towers residents shared a big win in the second prize. Jupiter's share was about £83. He invested most of his reward in a new suite of clothes and accessories, which he showed off when the TPA New Year's Day Sports procession marched off down Gill Street in January 1941.

Eunice Bowden remembered Jupiter from around this time when she used to accompany her grandfather Bill Stannard up town. She used to see Jupiter at the bus shed in front of the old town hall in Gill Street, where the old men of the Towers would congregate, especially on pension day. "Jupiter was well dressed in a black coat with a watch on it." She said he was a big heavy man. He smoked a pipe or something and he didn't say much. He didn't consider himself a black person. He was educated and had gone to England. "The old people would pat you on the head and say hold your hand out and they'd give you three pence." (Bowden: 17/10/2000)

In 1941, Jupiter was introduced to Home Affairs Minister Hanlon. He was the man who had made Jupiter's stay at Eventide possible. Hanlon described Jupiter as a polished old gentleman. Noted at this time was that Jupiter was the best-dressed man in the Home. He had dispensed with the old woollen jumper and tired pants that he had worn when he introduced to Prime Minister Joseph Lyons in 1937. Lyons visited a number of sites around the city that day in August, but ensured he spent time inspecting Eventide and meeting its most respected resident. Life at Eventide was good but quiet. Monotony and routine were broken by occasional concerts, performances and visitors. Beaty Landsberg played the piano for Jupiter. She'd venture up to the main administration building at Eventide from Blackheath College on Saturday mornings where Jupiter would sit and listen to her play. "He always gave me one of his paw-paws that he grew near his hut." (Landsberg: 26/10/2000)

Jupiter was also free to walk out to visit friends at Corinda on the outskirts of the city beyond Richmond Hill School. Allan Peno's family home at the far end of Prior Street was on Jupiter's way. He always called in to talk to Allan's grandfather. "He'd never come in though. He was polite, always 'Mrs' or 'Mr' and he was always well dressed. He had a hat and coat on. I'd listen to Grandad and Jupiter talking. They'd talk about horses and gold and that." (Peno: 20/10/2000)

Jupiter then walked on to the home of George and Minnie Boyd, who had lived on Jack Street to the east of the Waterworks Road from at least 1911. Most of the goldfield housing there had been removed, although close by lived George and Mona Bedford who were 'White' friends of Jupiter. Nearby lived the Masso, Johnson and Davidson families, and Cooper Kerr on country marked by the watershed of Sheepstation Creek to the west and Waterworks Road on the east. This dynamic of scattered housing was often used by family and friends visiting the city in the late 1930s. It lay in the shadow of the first 'Black's Camp' downstream from Buckland's slaughter yard. A number of children from the Kerr, Burdekin, Mackie, Dallachy, Amery and Boyd families attended Richmond Hill State School. (Brumby and Barrie) All of this changed when the war in the Pacific commenced in December 1941. Corinda was transformed into an airfield for use by the USAAF and all of the housing in the area above Peno's residence near MacPherson Street was removed. (TNM: 21/02/1947 – 2)

THE END

When Jupiter died on 6 December 1945, the establishment view was that his residence at Eventide had been "privileged by the government because of his historic association with the Towers". Jean Devanny's 'Bird of Paradise' was published the year Jupiter died. Devanny had interviewed Jupiter, along with others living in North Queensland, to appraise the impact of the Second World War on ordinary lives. The book's title came from when Jupiter spoke of his greatest reward, when asked by Devanny if he liked living at Eventide:

> "He picked up a little dove and stroked its silken feathers. Then, with half closed eyes and the gentlest of smiles, he turned to me. 'Missie! The spirit of freedom is like the bird of paradise in the jungle. It makes its home in the tops of the trees so it can feel the winds in its tails. But I like my little doves. If I am not about, they come to my room looking for me." (Devanny: 138)

The first generation of Europeans who had lived on Charters Towers since its beginnings had all but passed on, penultimately with Jupiter who was one of the poorest. He was followed ultimately by the wealthiest of them all. This was Sir Thomas Buckland, who died in Sydney on 11 June 1947, aged 99. Buckland was the businessman who had been in partnership in the slaughter yards on Sheep Station Creek in the 1880s that backdropped the lives of many Indigenous people leaving and entering the city.

Jupiter Mosman with a group of nurses readying for a street procession, Gill Street, 1941 – photographer unknown – Charters Towers Archives – 2007158.2847.

Prime Minister J.A. Lyons with Jupiter Mosman, Eventide Home, 1938 – photographer unknown – Charters Towers Archives – 2011192.7202.

CHAPTER NINETEEN
THE REUNIONS

Two years after the death of Jupiter, the number of Indigenous people living in the Charters Towers district had declined from 200 at the end of the Great War to 100. This excluded People who had been sent to Palm Island between 1901 and 1938, and People who had become exempt from living under the Act, as the take up of houses at Corinda in the 1930s attested to. Those exempted by 1948 included Jane Williams who had been released 1921, Charles Alley in 1933, Bob Roberts 1934, Malley 1931, Ada Reid 1939, Alwyn Kennedy 1941, Bobby Masso 1946, Henry Mitchell 1940, Cyril Patterson 1946, Nellie Smith Huen 1945 and Peter Purcell in 1945. (TNM: 21/02/1947) Some were exempted because, as cattle workers in northern Australia, they were essential to keeping up the supply to the meatworks and local butchers during and after the Second World War. It set about the opportunity to live in residences within the city of Charters Towers, often with the support of pastoralists.

The 75 year time-mark of the Charters Towers discovery was celebrated in 1947. This was spearheaded by 300 former residents being railed back to the city via a special train from Brisbane. These were the sons and daughters of the first pioneers, whose own departure some 40 years earlier changed the way the goldfield story could be told in Charters Towers. They would join with an expected "150 coloured people coming in from the district for the festivities in July..." (TNM: 01/05/1947 – 2) The problem for the Council however, was where to house the Indigenous people during their stay.

> "Since the end of the Second World War, the Aboriginal station worker had been scattered over various parts of the town, sometimes even in tents. For the past year the police had sent the Aboriginals, when in town, to a property formerly owned by the RAAF ... there were no sanitary provisions

> there and conditions generally were unsatisfactory. Mayor Cunningham gave the numbers as approximately 50 males, 15 females and 35 children." (TNM: 21/02/1947)

So in 1947, it was decided to re-purpose the old Australian Army detention barracks in upper Stubley Street that became known as The Reserve. The Reserve served as the post-war generation's home away from home for 30 years when people were allowed to visit the city for the Annual Show and for Christmas. The detention buildings and barbed wire had been removed in 1946, and while there was talk of erecting several small type buildings, including a communal kitchen, no action was taken at that time. Hence tent poles, ropes and canvas were walked or taxied up from the police station and erected on concrete remnants as accommodation. A cooking and laundry hut along with an ablution block were built in the 1950s, and electricity was finally laid on the late 1950s. (Babidge: 44)

MILLETT

In 1947, there were only fragments of written history at hand to recount to the expected influx of former Towersites. It was Richard Henry (Harry) Millet's *Glimpse of the Past* for The Northern Miner of 30th June 1947 that took on the task of helping the city remember. Rather than retelling George Clarke's story, Millett meshed Mines' Department accounts with newspaper accounts to which he added a dash of his own flavours:

> "In the latter part of 1871, Hugh Mosman, J. Fraser and G.E. Clarke discovered gold near the Gap. On January 2, 1872, Mosman travelled to Ravenswood and applied for the reward claims and a prospecting area and four men's ground was obtained from Commissioner Charters on January 26, 1872 on the North Australian line, near the Gap. Jupiter Mosman who was horse boy to Mosman and always declared that he found the gold, died at Eventide, Charters Towers, at 11.30 am on December 5, 1945. He was about 84 years of age. So rich was the surface gold that the returns for 1872 reached 31,287 oz, jumping to 74,746 oz for 1873. The field was named after Commissioner Charters, the 'towers' referring to the hills or "tors" which are a marked feature as one approaches to the city. The first store

> and hotel built on the Towers was the Royal. It was on the same ground as the present Royal hotel, and was owned by Owen and Woodburn (known as the two Joes)." (TNM:30/06/1947 – 3)

Millett's version was adopted by ongoing generations of Towersites, when one year later Town Clerk J.G. 'Jim' McClelland used Millett's story as the basis for an address to the Charters Towers Rotary Club on the topic of *Towers Goldfield: Discovery and Development.* This was published in The Northern Miner of 11 August 1948 and subsequently used verbatim two years later by Norman Dungavell in his ground-breaking book *Souvenir: Charters Towers 1872 to July 1950*. This publication coincided with another Back to Charters Towers event of that year. To Dungavell's credit, his compilation was the first attempt to go beyond the craft of reporting by the city's journalists and mining wardens to publish a reminiscence that belonged to the people. In his 1963 landmark study, *A Thousand Miles Away: A History of North Queensland to 1920,* academic historian Geoffrey Bolton used Dungavell's published work along with other sources to make this summation:

> "Late in 1871, Hugh Mosman, George Clarke and James Fraser joined forces to seek gold north of the Seventy Mile among a cluster of small peaks which they named Charters Tors in honour of the mining warden. As they prospected around the base of the hill, Mosman's 11-year-old Aboriginal boy Jupiter spied quartz outcrops thickly marked out with fine gold. At the end of January 1872, the party registered their claims at Ravenswood." (Bolton: 50)

Bolton's assessment brought Jupiter into the story as the gold finder, which he expressed using unladen language. He wisely excluded the circumstances that others had described that had brought about the discovery: from Jupiter seeking, looking or going for horses either on a dewy morning, during a storm or in dry times. Rather, he presented him possessing an eye for finding gold.

Jupiter Mosman – Norman Dungavell – *Souvenir: Charters Towers 1872 to July 1950* – Charters Towers Archives – 1950.

CHAPTER TWENTY
WILLIAMS MEMORIAL

Within weeks of Jupiter's passing in 1945, proposals were forwarded to raise a monument in his honour. Ideas included the building of a fountain and the naming of a park in Mosman Street. There was another to erect an obelisk with a granite ball and bronze tablet opposite the School of Arts. (At that time, Mayor John Cunningham thought it best to locate it on top of Towers Hill.) The likes of businessmen George Urquhart and Angus McCallum fund-raised while A.S. Cummings suggested reburying Jupiter in Lissner Park. The only thing lacking were sufficient funds to achieve any of these outcomes. This was particularly noteworthy, as the city was still held back by the same shortcomings to raise a memorial to the war dead from two world wars. This memorial to those who served was completed opposite the hospital for Armistice Day 1954.

In the meantime, local mining engineer Syd Williams set about building a memorial to Jupiter on his own account. He had a large gibber removed from Towers Hill and placed on a concrete plinth, replete with metal signage. This was erected in front of his residence, opposite the hospital in Gill Street in December 1953. Williams invited King Kiara, who was the last of the Dalleburra people, to unveil the Jupiter Mosman memorial. "We are fortunate to having a representative of the Dalleburra tribe in King Kiara living in our midst. The king lived at the time of this city's discovery. King Kiara son of Barney, King of the Dalleburra, stood in readiness, his brass plate reflecting the rays of the sun and a look of solemnity on his dignified countenance, one hand resting on top of his stick, for the king is now 88 years old. It was in perfect keeping with the occasion that this old king of a fast dying race should have been chosen to honour this one, who by his sterling personal qualifications of character deserves a niche in memory's halls when the annul of one of the most prosperous goldfields in Australia are under review." (TNM:18/02/1954 – 3) The plinth was inscribed with two statements:

> "This gibber was removed from the site of near 'The Gap' where 'Jupiter' 1861 – 1945 an aboriginal first discovered gold on Charters Towers Goldfield proclaimed 31/08/1872.
> Fine gold won 6,785,281 ounces to August 1947. Erected by Syd. N. Williams, Mining Engineer." [And on the other:] "Prospectors Hugh Mosman, George Clarke, J. Fraser and horse boy Jupiter were camped behind Towers Hill. During a heavy thunderstorm, the packhorses bolted and Jupiter tracked them to a gully near 'The Gap'. He stooped for a drink and when he put his head in the water he saw very rich specimens of gold ore. About 200 oz were found around the surface. Unveiled by King Kiara. Dedicated by Ald. R. Davies 24.12.1953."

Kiara was an interesting choice, that is, if a choice could be made. He had grown up on Flinders country rather than on the lands of the Burdekin. Kiara's father Barney had been accepted by Scottish-born Robert Christison soon after he took up Lammemoor to the south of Hughenden in 1862. (Loos: 49-50) Kiara said that he was born in 1866. Years later he moved to Oakley Station, which was another of Christison's properties and stayed there through changes in ownership. This led to him retiring to Charters Towers with Oakley's then last owner, the Johnson family, when they moved into business there in 1950. Kiara was happy living in the city with the Johnsons, even though he preferred to sleep in a humpy in their back yard. During the day he would stand outside Johnson's shop opposite the Court House Hotel in Gill Street. He could be seen by passersby wearing his king plate. 'King' Kiara Christison died on 6 January 1960, aged 80. (Claude Risdale: 11/03/2019) Kiara was chosen to do the unveiling by Williams and Davies because he linked directly to a 'tribe' and personified a tribal way of living; and besides, "the king lived at the time of this city's discovery." His role in the unveiling was supported by local Indigenous people who were in the city for Christmas.

CENTENARY MEMORIAL

For the purposes of compiling a more complete history of Charters Towers for its centenary in 1972, local woman Eleanor Springer embellished elements of the work of Millett, 'Kaz Yuel' and Bolton to manufacture a Yuletide fortune-adventure story for the city, titled 'A Glimpse of Glory': "They were accompanied by a young native lad who attached himself to Mosman, and to whom had been given the name Jupiter. It was a lucky day when they granted the boy's wish to join them for he repaid the kindness with a gift most coveted by man. So to Ravenswood, and in early 1871 the prospectors were surveying chances in the area. There they were joined by George Clarke, an experienced mining man. With youthful abandon, the group decided to prospect in areas which others considered impossible. Strangely, though, the secret could still have remained hidden, for the disgruntled and unhappy party wandered and sought unsuccessfully during many months. On the point of giving up, fate took a hand, and in a terrible thunderstorm the horses scattered, terror-stricken by vivid lightning and reverberating thunder. Jupiter, it was, who set out to track the missing animals. As he bent to drink at a clear stream, the dark-skinned youth saw the first of a treasure which would find a mighty city. Returning to his mates, he carried the gift to them — pure, sparkling gold — surely what must have been the richest Christmas gift ever, for the day was Christmas Day 1871." (Springer: 9-10)

What Jupiter recounted of that moment personally in 1939, and which never coincided with Christmas, is worth reiterating:

> "I had been out and found a nice piece of stone and went back to inform Hugh Mosman and he brought a pick and we dug it out, and I can assure you that is what started the mine called the North Australian." (TDB: 20/02/1939 –10)

It is simplicity in recount that would have worked in any retelling if Jupiter's letter to the editor of 1939 had been re-found at that time.

OTHER MONUMENTS

Sid Williams fully praised "Jupiter ... an aboriginal first discovered gold on Charters Towers Goldfield" with only cursory mention of the others in the discovery party. A second iteration took the form of a small concrete and stone cairn designed by local man John Banks to celebrate the city's centenary. This was erected on the site of the former North Australian mine in 1972. Local Indigenous man, Ken Kennedy, played the part of Jupiter in the opening ceremony, when he delivered a specimen of gold into the hands of the Governor of Queensland Sir Collin Hannah who then unveiled the cairn that carried the following inscription: "1872-1972 – This cairn marks the location of the finding of gold by Jupiter Mosman accompanying H. Mosman, J. Fraser, G. Clarke – December 1871 and official confirmation January 26th 1872."

In 1988, the gold discovery monument was erected in Centenary Park to celebrate the bicentenary of Australia. Tom Wyatt planned a landscape comprising a low grassed rise from which water slowly poured into a broad, rocky pool. Aside the pool, Wyatt set four sculptured metal figures created by Hugh Anderson to recreate the discovery moment of 1871: one of the men holding the reins of a laden horse; in front, a man working a gold pan beside the pool; and on the other side, a more youthful figure kneeling beside the water, holding up a large stone to his face. As a concept by local identity Henry Weare, it cut through with George Clarke not being present at that time; showed John Fraser with a pack horse; Hugh Mosman using a gold pan in an attempt to find specs in the top end of Mosman Creek; and a young Jupiter away from the rest, having "been out and found a nice piece of stone..." (TDB: 20/02/1939 – 10)

Williams Memorial, Gill Street – photographer unknown – Charters Towers Archives – Charters Towers Archives – 2008171.3287.38 Jupiter Memorial.

King Kiara at the Charters Towers Hospital, 1952 – photographer unknown – Charters Towers Archives – 2009175.3515.

CHAPTER TWENTY-ONE
JUPITER MOSSMAN SOCIETY

After 1945, a number of families were living in the city on a full-time basis, especially as exemptions from living under the Act increased, and work became available as domestics at boarding colleges or on the City or Shire Council, etc. School records demonstrate this move to permanent living in Charters Towers. Children from the Alley, Saturday, Boyd, Kennedy, Davidson and later the McLean families were taught at Richmond Hill School from 1947 onwards, while Crowley, Kerr, Burdekin, Sailor, Saturday, Johnson, Kerwin, Masso and Blackman families enrolled at Central State School.

Conversely, numbers in the bush declined, as trucking replaced droving and equal wages squeezed extra workers off cattle stations. In 1975, the Reserve on upper Stubley Street closed when the area was declared a health risk. The Department of Aboriginal and Islander Advancement (D.A.I.A.) moved everyone off and burnt the buildings. (Babidge: 44) The closure was a decisive act, in which all Indigenous people were to live inside Charters Towers rather than on the fringe. This was largely brought about by the Commonwealth Government's new policy on self-determination. In this light, the Queensland Government, through the D.A.I.A., played a role in buying and building at least seven houses, mainly in the Millchester State School catchment, to address this change.

The transformation to city dweller received the greater support — clearly as an act of self-determination — from the Jupiter Mossman Housing Community Cooperative Society. A founding member of the Society, Harriet Hulthern, believes it formed in 1973 with members of the Alberts, Reid and Mitchell families and others being involved in finding more secure accommodation for Indigenous families. At this time, 28 families became financial members of the Society. It was incorporated in April 1975, with eight older houses purchased and renovated with plans to build another three. The Society charged low rent for their housing which, like D.A.I.A. houses, were scattered throughout the city. (Society occupancy rules, however, were less strict.) Current housing stocks stand at 39. This assists to accommodate some of the 1,033 Aboriginal and/or Torres Strait Islander people counted at the 2016 census living in the Charters Towers Region who make up 9% of all people living here. (Slowman; Hulthern; ABS 2016 Census)

Hence there is a high level of success in First Nations people being accommodated, even though one senses a cry-out for greater social and economic advantage, which is still beyond the author's personal calling to unravel. At least now there is a place in history for their story through Jupiter Mosman to have been assembled and now shared.

Jupiter Mosman's grave, Charters Towers Cemetery, 1971.

APPENDIX A

Diane Menghetti's 1984 PhD history thesis *Charter Towers* unwisely postulated the circumstances that led to Jupiter becoming a member of the discovery party. In a postscript to her thesis, Menghetti explained: "Hugh Mosman was married to an aboriginal woman whom the rate books showed living in a bark hut in the unsurveyed area of the town. It is my opinion that Jupiter was Hugh Mosman's son." (Menghetti) Menghetti's opinion was based solely on her reading of the Charters Towers City Council Valuation Register of 1877. (The marriage was not registered with Births Deaths and Marriages in Queensland.) Its listings included a two-room slab and iron hut on land east of Mosman Creek which was in the name of 'Mrs H. Mosman'. Menghetti concluded that a woman who was seemingly housed in a primitive hut away from the mainstream of the one square mile belonged to a lesser class. At the very least she was a kept woman and at the most she was an Indigenous woman.

Closer scrutiny of the valuation register of 1877 revealed a deeper story about women living within the Charters Towers municipality at that time. It shows 'Mrs H. Mosman' was one of only four women who paid rates on land and property within the one square mile, where in fact she was one of only two who owned the house she occupied. All the rest of the rate payers were men. So regardless of the primitive architecture, Mrs Mosman was a woman of some note and perhaps importance. What was not registered were the Indigenous people who lived within the one square mile on unsurveyed allotments. About 200 of them were camped over the creek at the rear of Arthur Callcott's humpy in 1875. Such a camp would not have included a woman living in a slab and iron hut, because their means of living and accommodation were less substantial than Mrs Mosman's. The other point is that the camp in question was in another direction from Mosman Creek, both socially and geographically from where 'Mrs H. Mosman' lived.

So if Mrs H. Mosman was not of Aboriginal descent, then who was she? She was Hugh Mosman's mother, Mrs Harriet Mosman. She was a 56-year-old widow of independent means, whose husband Archibald had died 14 years earlier in Sydney. With the exception of her youngest daughter Alice then aged 15, all of her children had grown up. Harriet Mosman spent time living in the north to be close to her sons until she passed away in London in 1883. Diane Menghetti believed family mattered and accounted for Jupiter being with Hugh Mosman because he was his son rather than having been 'acquired'. Family mattered when telling Jupiter's story, even if he had never married.

ABBREVIATIONS

ABS	Australian Bureau of Statistics
BC	Brisbane Courier
C (R)	Courier (Rockhampton)
CBE	Cleveland Bay Express
C&C	Cummins and Campbells Magazine
DNA	Daily Northern Argus (Rockhampton)
GMC	Gold Mining Company
HFD	Hann Family Diary
JMF	Jupiter Mosman File
MMSKA	Mackay Mercury and South Kennedy Advertiser
NMR	Northern Mining Register
NQR	North Queensland Register
Q	Queenslander
GGG	Queensland Government Gazette
QSA	Queensland State Archives
QT	Queensland Times
RM	Ravenswood Miner
SMH	Sydney Morning Herald
TB	Townsville Bulletin
TDB	Townsville Daily Bulletin
TET	The Evening Telegraph
TM	The Mercury
TNM	The Northern Miner
V&P	Votes and Proceedings

SOURCES

NON-PRINT AND PRINT

PRIMARY

Australian Institute of Aboriginal and Torres Strait Islander Studies, Canberra

Annual Reports of the Northern Protector of Aboriginals, 1899–1903.

Annual Reports of the Chief Protector of Aboriginals, 1904–1916.

*Reports Upon the Operations of Certain Sub-Departments of the Home Secretary's Departmen*t – Aboriginals Department, 1918–1939.

Native Affairs, 1940–1959.

https://aiatsis.gov.au/collection/featured-collections/remove-and-protect

Department of Natural Resources, Cloncurry

White Hills Run A/63751 PH 2657 White Hills Part 1.

White Hills File 2657 White Hills Part 2.

Department of Aboriginal and Torres Strait Islander Policy and Development, Brisbane

Jupiter Mosman Personal File (8J/91).

James Cook University

Hann Family Archive: H/1-H/17 Diaries.

Queensland Police Museum, Brisbane

Lake Nash File.

Archibald Mosman Personal File.

Archibald Mosman Staff File AF 1093 at A/40056).

Queensland State Archives, Brisbane

QSA: COL 321 – Eventide – Correspondence Re: Waiting Lists 1929– 1941.

QSA: ID846794, Correspondence – Inwards: 301 – 600COL/A64, 499 of 1865 – Bowen to Col Sec., 13/12/1865.

QSA: PR846759 Inward correspondence no. 62/1428.

QSA: 75680, 75677.

QSA: 846794.
State Library of Queensland, Brisbane
Ernest Eglington, *A Few Rambling Notes of Happenings in the Far North West of Queensland 40 to 45 Years Ago.* [typescript] 1920.
Sir Thomas McIllwraith/ Palmer Papers.
Charters Towers Archives, Charters Towers
North Queensland Register's Mining History of Charters Towers 1872 to 1897, North Queensland Register, 1897.
Correspondence with Newington College, Sydney, 08/12/1998.
Correspondence with Kings College, Parramatta, 1994.
Correspondence with John Pohl, 26/11/2019.
Magazines
Cummins and Campbells Magazine.
Memoirs
Michael Cunningham, *Pioneering of the River Burdekin, Brisbane,*1895.
Frank Hann's *Lolworth Diaries 1866–1875,* Hesperian Press, 2013.
Newspapers
Brisbane Courier
Courier (Rockhampton)
Cleveland Bay Express
Cummins and Campbells Magazine
Daily Northern Argus (Rockhampton)
Mackay Mercury and South Kennedy Advertiser
Northern Mining Register
Queenslander
Queensland Times
Ravenswood Miner
Townsville Bulletin
Townsville Daily Bulletin
The Evening Telegraph
The Mercury
The Northern Miner
Oral History
Eunice Bowden, 17/10/2000
Harriet Hulthern, 18/6/2021
Beattie Landsberg, 26/10/2000

Bob Mark, 06/03/1999
Alan Peno, 20/10/2000
John Pohl, 26/11/2019
Claude Risdale, 11/03/2019
Glen Sowman, 17/06/2021
Queensland Government Gazette
Votes and Proceedings

SECONDARY

An Australian Post Office History: Charters Towers.

Anne Allingham, *Taming the Wilderness,* James Cook University, 1878.

Anne Allingham, *A Rare and Exceptional Bowl, North Queensland, 2008.* http://www.sothebys.com/en/auctions/ecatalogue/2008/aboriginal-art-au0721/lot.28.html

Sally Babidge, *Written True Not Gammon: a History of Aboriginal Charters Towers,* Black Ink Press, 2007.

Sally Babidge, *Aboriginal Family and the State: the Conditions of History,* Routledge, 2016

Mary Montgomerie Bennett, *Christison of Lammermoor,* Alston Rivers, 1927.

Geoffrey Bolton, *A Thousand Miles Away: a History of North Queensland to 1920,* Jacaranda, 1963.

E.J. Brady, *The Land of the Sun,* Edward Arnold, 1924.

Michael Brumby, *Black to Gold,* Charters Towers Archives, 2014.

Charters Towers: *The City it Was, The City It Is, the City it's Going to Be 1872–1922,* Towers Jubilee Committee, 1922.

Celebrating the Centenary of Boulia: Capital of the Channel Country Queensland, 1976.

Edward M Curr, *The Australian Race: Its Origin, Languages, Customs, Place of Landing in Australia and the Routes By Which It Spread Itself Over That Continent,* John Farnes Government Printer 1886.

Brian Dalton (editor), *News From Nulla: Correspondence of Rebecca and George Cain, 1866–7,* Dpt History and Politics, James Cook University, 1991.

Jean Devanny, *Bird of Paradise,* Johnson, 1945.

Hudson Fysh, *Taming the North: The Story of Alexander Kennedy and Other Queensland Pathfinders,* Angus and Robertson, 1933.

Matthew Fox (editor), *History of Queensland,* States Publishing, 1919.

Robert Gray, *Reminiscences of India and North Queensland, 1857–1912,* Constable, 1913.

W.R.O. Hill, *Forty Five Years' Experiences in North Queensland,* Pole, 1907.

Janette Holcomb, *Early Merchant Families of Sydney: Speculation and Risk Management on the Fringes of Empire,* Anthem Press, 2014.

Robert Logan Jack, *Report on the Geology and Mineral Resources of the District Between Charters Towers Goldfield's and the Coast,* Brisbane, GSQ, 1879.

W. Ross Johnston, *The Long Blue Line: A History of the Queensland Police,* Brisbane, Booralong, 1992.

North Queensland Register's Mining History of Charters Towers, 1872 to 1897.

Elena Springer (editor), *Charters Towers Centenary 1872–1972,* 1972.